Foreword

By JOSEPHINE BARNES

DBE, MA, DM, FRCP, FRCS, FRCOG, Hon. FRCPI, MD, DM, D.Sc.

*Consulting Obstetrician and Gynaecologist, Charing Cross Hospital
and Elizabeth Garrett Anderson Hospital
Past President, British Medical Association*

This is a book written by a woman for women. Joan Jenkins is the co-ordinator of Women's Health Concern, a charity which is devoted to the special problems that women face during the phases of their lives.

It is a sad reflection on the British National Health Service that, while in most ways it provides excellent care in serious illness, it often fails to get to grips with those conditions defined by doctors as 'minor ailments', but which can cause distress, disruption of family life and sometimes loss of employment for women. This is to some degree a reflection on the education received by medical students. There tends to be an undue emphasis on 'rare' and 'interesting' conditions and on the dramas of medicine. Fortunately in many medical schools these shortcomings are being recognised and a new approach — which may be described as 'patient orientated' — is emerging.

Nevertheless it is true that many women are singularly ill-informed about the workings of their own bodies or of the disturbances in normal function — as distinct from frank disease — that may be experienced. But this book has to indicate the difficulties that many women experience in their dealings with their doctors. General Practitioners may be overworked and overwhelmed by too many people with trivial complaints. But through apathy, and lack of interest or knowledge some — but by no means all — fail to give to their women patients the sympathetic understanding and a simple explanation which is often all that is needed.

This book answers very many of the questions women ask and indicates when and where treatment should be sought. Its list of useful addresses in the United Kingdom and world-wide will help many to get the help which they may feel they lack.

There is no doubt that thousands of women will have good cause to be grateful for this book and thus indebted to its author, Joan Jenkins.

CARING FOR WOMEN'S HEALTH

CARING FOR WOMEN'S HEALTH

JOAN JENKINS

WOMEN'S HEALTH CONCERN
in association with
SEARCH PRESS

First published 1985
by WOMEN'S HEALTH CONCERN
Limited by guarantee
Registered Charity No. 279651
17 Earls Terrace
London W8 6LP
in association with
SEARCH PRESS LTD.

ISBN 0 906848 07 5 (paperback)

ISBN 0 85532 554 2 (hardback)

Typeset by EN–TO–EN Ltd., Tunbridge Wells, Kent
Printed in Great Britain by
Biddles Ltd, Guildford, Surrey

Contents

Author's Preface

Health has now become an increasingly 'popular' subject for media coverage, and women generally have become much more aware of possible health hazards. For many, however, there still remains a huge gap of ignorance about their problems and about women's specific ills. Many of them also tend to neglect their own basic health care. There is a vital need for reliable information on these subjects.

Women's Health Concern (WHC), a registered charity in Britain, provides information and advice to all those who seek its help with their health problems. WHC concentrates mainly on gynaecological conditions and its medical experts in this field try to help doctors to look at women's health problems seriously and to treat them with appropriate medical or other suitable treatment, whether their symptoms are caused by physical or psychological illness (or both) — or by emotional distress.

One of the ways in which Women's Health Concern achieves this is by publishing a series of booklets, written by doctors and other experts, on such subjects as *Feminine Hygiene, Premenstrual Syndrome and Period Pains, Post-Natal Depression, The Menopause* and *Sexually Transmitted Diseases*. The texts of these five booklets are included in the particular chapters in Part II of this book; and if there are occasional repetitions of facts and advice in this book, it is deliberate so that these specialist chapters can be read complete in themselves.

WHC does not publish booklets on childbirth or contraception because there are many good publications which are available from other charities and organisations on these subjects; but the work of WHC's medical advisers and colleagues in their hospitals and practices covers, of course, every aspect of women's health care.

I have worked since 1972 to establish and develop WHC and its services and to communicate up-to-date facts of women's health problems to women themselves. There is still a long way to go before the public at large can be properly educated on all aspects of health care and health problems, but Women's Health Concern has already helped many thousands of women to enjoy healthier and more worthwhile lives. I hope this book will reach and help many thousands more.

Acknowledgments

I take this opportunity to express my gratitude to the directors, advisers, medical colleagues and friends of Women's Health Concern. I am especially indebted to Dr Gerald Swyer whose expert knowledge and long experience in the field of women's health has provided the organisation with the guidance it needed to communicate soundly based advice and opinions to the benefit of countless health sufferers and well women, many of whom were 'in the dark' with their own problems. I also thank the writers and broadcasters who contributed the first positive articles and radio and television programmes on those subjects, information on which I was disseminating for public understanding in the early 1970s.

The foundation stones for the charity, Women's Health Concern (limited by guarantee) and still to be known as WHC, were truly laid by 1979. The initial grant was donated by Langham Life Assurance Company Limited — £10,000 — and this was a God-sent blessing at that time. Since then we are indebted to companies, trusts, individuals and to the DHSS for donations and grants that have enabled the charity to pursue the health education activities to which its members are dedicated. I thank the counsellors, particularly the occupational health nurses; the helpers who have kept WHC records and those who have despatched huge piles of letters on many occasions. I am also grateful to my son, Glyn, who has given so much time to driving me many miles in pursuance of WHC missions. My effort could not have been sustained and this book would not have been written without their support.

Joan Jenkins
May 1984

Ground Floor
17 Earls Terrace
London W8 6LP

Women's health — a gap in knowledge and understanding

One of the advantages of being an older woman in the 1980s is that I can reflect on women's attitudes to their health in the past. In my childhood during the 1930s the women were just as varied and individual as they are today but, on the whole, they were more resourceful and they were also the loving focal point of family life. They were brought up principally with marriage in mind, yet with little understanding of what they might expect from a good sexual relationship. One aspect of their lives which puzzled me even then was the general acceptance that women's recurring health problems were natural but untreatable. Few women, even outstanding characters, seemed to question this and few doctors tried to help with medication. Discussion of menstrual pains, let alone the menopause, was taboo and most women expected to be 'old' by forty. I grew up determined not to become one of these, but my questions remained unanswered until many years later and then they became crucial to my intention of forming the organisation which is now known as Women's Health Concern (WHC).

In the 1940s many young women in Britain took on a new role as members of the armed forces and in factories. I chose to become a nurse, but this made me even more concerned by the glaring gap in the treatment of women's health problems. Nor did there seem to be much concern or understanding of the psychological aspects. In the crowded sixty-bed women's ward in the hospital where I worked — which included women who were suffering from all kinds of diseases as well as gynaecological illnesses — only rarely did the patients or their relatives ask for a doctor's explanation, and young student nurses like myself were definitely not supposed to talk to them about their health problems.

During the 1950s and 1960s the world was awakening to new ideas and the Women's Liberation Movement was pointing out some of the faults in social structures. But in most women's knowledge of gynaecological problems the gap continued. By then I had become absorbed, over an eight-year period, in my work as a member of a specialist film unit that was producing a very successful series of post-graduate medical teaching films which were, in fact, the first of their kind to be made in colour. This experience enriched my knowledge of the human body; and further work

11

on documentary films for industry and travel films for the cinema widened my knowledge of people and took me to locations in most European countries and the United States. I then spent four years in television and radio before I became involved in the projection of two traditional women's organisations — first as Press Officer to The Girl Guides Association and then as Public Relations Consultant for the National Federation of Womens Institutes. Both these movements were anxious to sustain their old roots but simultaneously to develop new ideas. At that time I followed with special attention the progress of the Women's Liberation groups but it seemed to me that they paid too little attention to the real differences between men and women and I was disappointed by their apparent lack of knowledge about the common cyclic difficulties that are experienced by most women at some time or another in their lives.

Endocrinology, the study of the endocrine or ductless glands and their secretions, the hormones, had made considerable progress since the first chemical identification of a hormone about 1930 and the development of the first synthetic hormone in 1938. The term 'hormone' had been coined by Bayliss and Starling in 1902 to apply to the substance called 'secretin'. Secretin is secreted by the intestine into the blood stream and causes secretion of the pancreatic juice that is particularly involved in the digestion of proteins. There are a number of endocrine glands in the body and these include the pancreas, the thyroid gland, the testes in men, and the ovaries in women which secrete the female sex hormones — oestrogen and progesterone. Knowledge of endocrinology has made it possible for doctors to treat problems of hormone imbalance and this includes oestrogen deficiency which is suffered by many women during and after the menopause, and in other gynaecological conditions.

The 1950s was an historic era also in the development of the use of the contraceptive pill — the first trials were made in 1954 and the first prescriptions were given to women in Britain in 1960. By the early 1970s, however, it was becoming clear that women who received properly prescribed modern treatments were in a different class of health and well-being from those who were left to suffer their symptoms untreated. This latter situation was caused either because doctors failed to recognise the source of these problems or because they believed them to be a necessary part of a woman's life. Many doctors ignored the medical advances that had been made and some women were not anxious to try modern treatment anyway. The doctors who were not interested in endocrinology at that time had been taught in their medical schools that treatment with oestrogens had caused cancer in *mice* — a conclusion that had been reached from the early tests. That was apparently all they wanted to know, so they prescribed other treatments for women who were often suffering the genuine symptoms of common problems. Most women remained ignorant about the anatomy and physiology of their own bodies (in simple terms anatomy is what is and physiology is what it does). The huge gap of ignorance and neglect in this field, therefore, could only be filled over a long period by new schemes of education and training for both doctors and women.

A number of organisations and charities in Britain had been working to educate women about contraception and about caring for themselves and their babies. These included the Marie Stopes Clinic, The National Childbirth Trust and, of course, The Family Planning Association (FPA). The Health Education Council (HEC) had also been set up by government funding in 1968 to provide information to the public.**

At that time I was offered a medical assignment with an international pharmaceutical organisation which had supported extensive medical research over many years to develop oestrogen/progestogen therapy for menopause problems. This gave me the opportunity to study the subject thoroughly and to meet the top medical experts working in this field. It also heightened my determination to try to work out a communication project that would help the public with personalised information and advice on gynaecological subjects and in particular on women's cyclic problems. In 1972 I issued a press release about the menopause and its possible treatment by scientifically approved medicine. It gave journalists their first reliable information on the subject and some enlightened articles and radio and television programmes about the menopause began to appear in 1973. It also marked the beginning of what later became Women's Health Concern.

The next few years were busy, exciting and shattering ones. First, it was difficult to obtain funds to start a suitable organisation. It was also difficult to find colleagues able to devote enough of their time and energy to help to develop the organisation. We continued to disseminate and publicise facts about women's health problems and answered many thousands of letters and inquiries from women of all ages and social classes. I was invited to take part in radio and television programmes. I talked to women's meetings in Britain, and when I was lucky enough to visit four African countries – Ghana, Nigeria, Kenya and Tanzania – I met doctors, nurses and health workers and was able to see for myself some of the vast problems they faced in their health care scenes. This made me more aware of the fact that Western society tends to take for granted the social benefits it derives from modern technology and scientific advances: for instance, the provision of clean water, sewerage disposal systems, adequate nutrition and the almost complete eradication of diseases such as small pox and poliomyelitis.

In Britain, I worked in close liaison with medical research teams in post-graduate teaching hospitals, and slowly the first menopause clinics started to function in gynaecological departments in hospitals in London, in Birmingham and in Leeds; but the money needed for these clinics came for the most part from pharmaceutical companies who were financing clinical trials.

Our first organisation, The Association for Women's Health Care

---

**See Appendix 1 for a list of useful organisations.

(limited by guarantee) was established in 1977 in premises in an eighteenth-century house in London's West End. On 18 August 1978 *The Guardian* reported 'the fact that attitudes are at last changing is at least partly due to the work of Women's Health Care . . .'

But this organisation was destroyed that very month because of adverse publicity against the modest contributions it received from five pharmaceutical companies. Articles in *The General Practitioner* magazine and in two national newspapers, *The Guardian* and the *Sunday Times*, as well as a television *World in Action* programme, made preposterous attacks upon our sponsors on the grounds that they were giving financial support to our organisation in order to promote financial gains for themselves. This was considered by the people who knew the facts to be unfair. Our work had been governed by six prestigious medical consultants who were members of our Board of Directors, and there was no question of any bias or influence from the pharmaceutical industry. At that time it had not been possible to obtain funds from anywhere else to get our organisation started. I saw no sensible reason why it should have been otherwise because the vital information that had been assembled by research workers carrying out clinical medical trials about specific women's illnesses had been financed by the pharmaceutical industry. In fact, without them and their research funds the world would be without many of the benefits it has derived from using scientifically tested and approved medical treatments. But, alas, the truth has so often been distorted by the publicity.

In hindsight, however, it was fortunate that we were being made to think again about the best way to continue the work we had begun. There was no question of destroying the wealth of good will and the progress we had made. There had been much favourable publicity about our work and thousands of letters still continued to come to us for help and advice.

The upshot was that in 1979 a small group of medical consultants, a publisher, a legal adviser, an accountant and myself came together to create a new organisation which was constituted under the name of Women's Health Concern (WHC). We succeeded in obtaining a grant of £10,000 from an insurance company and this, together with the combination of professional skills and persistent hard work, enabled this organisation to be properly structured as a national charity in Britain in 1980. I agreed to be its co-ordinator. Dr Gerald Swyer became its first Chairman and WHC Medical Advisers were appointed in Wales and Scotland. By then there were also many other consultant gynaecologists, and other specialists and doctors in Britain and elsewhere, who were always willing to see women referred to them by their doctors. This wide network of WHC experts made it possible for us to help women in many places, so much so that WHC became known as 'the national sorting house for women's health problems'. However, Women's Health Concern's future success depended upon the charity getting sufficient funds and support to develop the organisation to do the work that was needed. By

1984 WHC had become indebted to many donors and had received three administrative grants from the Department of Health and Social Security (DHSS) which recognised the importance of the work it had to do.

The role of Women's Health Concern

The principal aim of WHC is to help women obtain information and personal advice concerning their health and related problems. It also publishes booklets on specific women's health subjects and it assists in arranging meetings and symposia for doctors and nurses.

For example, in order to help nurses and doctors talk to women sufferers about their problems – in particular, the premenstrual syndrome (PMS) commonly called PMT, the menopause, and post-natal depression – WHC in liaison with St Thomas' Hospital Medical School (Department of Obstetrics and Gynaecology) ran a pilot series of ten courses in London from January 1980 to November 1981 and two joint medical teaching symposia for doctors and occupational health nurses in January 1982 and in April 1983. They were entitled 'The Health of Women at Work' and covered a range of subjects including: dysmenorrhoea and menhorrhagia (period problems); migraine and headache; mastectomy (breast operation) and its after-care; the pregnant woman at work; before and after hysterectomy; the menopause and later; PMS; nutritional and immunological factors in women's health; breast and cervical screening programmes; and disorders specific to certain jobs.

The biggest problem for women in general has always been the question of how to obtain reliable information. From its outset WHC has sought to provide up-to-date and known facts about specific gynaecological problems and offers advice about all kinds of illness. It also tries to sort out some of the misunderstandings that arise between women and their doctors, and to help both towards a better understanding of the problems. We often find ourselves at the end of a chain for those who have been made aware of certain health hazards by articles and programmes and have then sought help for themselves in different directions including local health authorities, women's committees and groups and, of course, their own doctors. Doctors tend to be suspicious of information that has been acquired outside the medical profession and, unfortunately, many women who try to talk to them about a problem that might be referred to as 'pop journalists' nonsense' have been dismissed without proper attention or advice. As a result some women have grown to mistrust their doctors and throw away prescriptions they are given.

Many of the inquiries come to WHC from women who are well informed but who need specialist advice. At the same time we have to listen and respond to those who are just starting to look at themselves and who need sensitive and informed guidance. A typical conversation sometimes goes as follows: 'I don't know if you can help me . . .' The menopause, PMT, 'Baby Blues' or one of the other problems that is receiving publicity at the time is then mentioned as a possible cause for whatever is wrong. She goes on: 'I've been to see my doctor who doesn't seem to want to know about it' or 'I don't want to see any more doctors . . . where can I go to near my home to talk to someone who really understands?'

These women have usually heard about WHC from a friend, a doctor or nurse, from another organisation, or one of the well known 'agony aunties' from newspapers, magazines, radio or television. Some of them will have been categorised by doctors as those who fill their waiting rooms when they are not really ill. Women, more than men, are likely to visit doctors when they have symptoms of ill-health and especially for problems of a psychological nature like anxiety and depression, whether from social or personal factors.

Some of the most worrying cases are the women who feel they are being a nuisance and sometimes they are the ones who continue to suffer genuine symptoms and illness without consulting doctors. On the other hand, doctors constantly ponder on how to eliminate unnecessary consultations without, at the same time, increasing the level of serious illness that goes untreated.

It is also true that writers and broadcasters have not always been interested in the fact that most doctors' work is successful and appreciated. Complaints against doctors and the health services make, unfortunately, dramatic 'copy' for journalists writing commentaries on medical matters; and investigations by The Consumers' Association, for example, about patients' dislikes are also favourite topics. However some complaints about doctors are justified and some are not. Genuine complaints must be taken seriously and they can help good doctors to become better doctors but they should never be used to attack the medical profession as a whole. For it is true, regrettably, that since the mid-1970s a tendency towards anti-doctor propaganda has shown itself in press, radio and television channels.

Sometimes the women we have managed to help send letters of gratitude, like this one:

'Just to say thank you for talking to me. I can't tell you how much better you made me feel. I was frightened of myself and very desperate and if I hadn't found out about WHC just then I really don't know what I would have done . . . Thank you for being there.'

A vast amount of work has been done. A vast amount still remains to be done.

PART 1

Women and the health care scene

CHAPTER I

Social changes that have affected women's life-style

It is not possible to consider seriously women's present lives and the changing pattern of family life without some reference to history and to women, past and present, in countries and cultures different to our own.

When Queen Victoria came to the throne in Britain in 1837 women had few rights. They had no vote, and when they married, their possessions, including their children, belonged to the husband. The Matrimonial Causes Act of 1857, concerned with divorce, was the first statutory act of protection for the property of married women; the Married Women's Property Act of 1870 enabled married women to receive independent benefits: on their own earnings up to £200; a further Married Women's Property Act of 1882 removed the husband's automatic rights to his wife's property; the Matrimonial Causes Act of 1884 gave the wife rights over her own person. In 1925 the Law of Property Act gave official recognition to the view that the husband and wife should be treated as two separate individuals in any property transaction. The Law Reform Act of 1935 and the Married Women (restraint upon Anticipation) Act of 1949 cleared away the last restrictions. At the same time changes in the contract law were made which enabled the wife to contract in her own name. Further improvements were made with regard to parental rights and divorce and gradually the laws for separation and maintenance have been changed in order to give equal rights to both sexes.

The Feminist movement was born in the Victorian middle-class drawing room and not in the factory. At the beginning it was the outcome of a middle-class problem that affected the many women who did not get married because they outnumbered the eligible men. These spinsters were regarded as a nuisance in society because they were lacking in education and could only earn small wages mainly as governesses or as needle-women stitching seams. At the same time, many married women were not adequately protected by their husbands' earnings. Tens of thousands of wretched women at that time were forced into prostitution or faced with the threat of being sent to the work-house and the disgrace of losing class when they were no longer able to support themselves. Families were large by the end of the nineteenth century, and marriage for the unfortunate daughters often meant going into a matrimonial cage with a selfish man who took advantage of his wife's dependence on him. The role of women was still to be subservient to men who were their masters and the rulers of the family.

The movement for the emancipation of women gathered force. Its beginnings were not so much political as economic and educational. By the end of the nineteenth century endowed schools for girls had been set up and despite much opposition the universities had been breached – between 1869 and 1881 Girton and Newnham colleges were founded at Cambridge and Lady Margaret Hall and Somerville at Oxford, but it was some years later that they were accorded equal status with men's colleges. The State System of education began officially in 1870 and included the education of girls. The Education Act of 1902 enabled local authorities to maintain and assist secondary education for both sexes. By 1920, 185,000 girls were receiving secondary education in Britain and by 1939 there were more than 500,000. The increased education for women meant that they had better opportunities to earn more money and, for many, the future was beginning to look much more hopeful.

The pioneer work of the early suffragettes was also of vital importance. The Women's Suffrage Committee was set up in 1886 but received no genuine support from governments until after 1905 when Mrs Pankhurst had founded the Women's Social and Political Union. Their struggle continued into the First World War when public attitudes began to change because women had to take on men's work in factories and elsewhere. After the end of the war in 1918 a bill was passed giving the vote to men over 21 and women over 30. In 1928 all women over 21 were given the vote.

The legal position of women is greatly improved as compared with 150 years ago, particularly within marriage where the husband has not only lost proprietory rights over his wife's person and property, but has become liable to proceedings for divorce and the custody of the children, must leave his deserted wife in the matrimonial home and may not exercise the common law right of 'reasonable chastisement'.

Since the 1950s family life has sometimes been regarded as no longer the norm. Nevertheless most families still comprise married couples with children who are dependent on the husband's income which is often supplemented by the wife's earnings. More women now go out to work in Britain than in any other European country. About 56 per cent of married women were working in the early 1980s. It is generally accepted throughout the world, including in some traditional strongholds in the Third World, that women who are able to spend at least part of their time at work outside their homes are healthier in mind and body than those who stay all the time at home.

Women at work experience the same stresses and strains as men but most of them learn to deal with this for themselves. The biological differences between the sexes, however, obviously cause different problems. For instance, about 55 per cent of pregnant women continue to work for the first six months or longer of their pregnancies. Of these, 35 per cent work in offices, 25 per cent in personal services – which includes shops, hairdressers and restaurants – 15 per cent in health and education, while the remainder do casual jobs or freelance work. Because of nausea and morning sickness 25 per cent of them need time off during the first three months and others suffer hypertension and other health hazards. Job efficiency is reduced for 47 per cent of them. Those who work in jobs that entail standing for long periods are in danger of having small babies. They are entitled to claim a limited amount of money from the National Health Service (NHS) maternity benefits. If they have worked for more than two years in one job they have the right to return to that job within a certain time limit. But it is becoming more difficult for women to find jobs these days – especially those who have no professional qualifications or trained skills, while women in some areas of employment are still paid less than men for doing similar work.

Some women will always find much of their life's fulfilment in their roles as wives and mothers and they try to develop interests for themselves and for their families in the world they build around them. Most children no longer get the loving care and support that was given for many years by grand mothers and other relatives, but there are compensations for the loss of extended family support. For instance, the *sensible* use of television and radio can be a wonderful asset. The local swimming pool provides health-giving exercise as well as the opportunity to socialise and there are many more facilities for taking part in indoor and outdoor sports. The lists of activities available is almost unending. Also more people are now travelling to other countries for holidays and work and are able to take part in all sorts of activities that were not available to them in the past.

An increasing number of women now cope with their family lives as well as some kind of work and leisure interest. It is important that they obtain sufficient exercise, of course, which is why, for example, Yoga has become more popular. Many women attend classes to learn about good breathing and how they can help themselves to relax after a hard day's work. Yoga also claims to help to relieve pressure on their internal organs and to maintain good muscle tone throughout the body.

A person's life-style obviously depends on many factors: health, age, intelligence, means, how busy one is, what responsibilities one has, where one lives and the knowledge one has managed to acquire beyond formal education. For those who suffer ill-health, however, and those who live in poverty there is little joy.

Some women regard themselves as isolated, frustrated and even deprived by their family lives. Loneliness, environmental discomfort and lack of help with children and ageing relatives has always caused anxiety and suffering. Too much stress can sometimes be the reason why they become addicted to drugs, alcohol, excessive smoking or over-eating. Neglect of themselves and possibly of their children too, and the inability or difficulties they may have in seeking medical, social and legal advice can create further problems.

Feminists have been calling for more nurseries, increased child benefits, shared parenting, shared jobs, better housing and welfare, adequate contraception and abortion facilities, shelters for battered women, rape crisis and other resource centres for women. Some of them are seeking fundamental social changes which they believe could integrate work, family life and community.

Although more people than ever are marrying today, the rate of divorce is high – present trends in Britain show it to be about one in three. But marriage is still believed, by most, to provide the only sure security for pregnant women and their children so long as it can be properly worked out between a couple. At the same time, the social stigma for unmarried mothers has almost disappeared since the 1970s and more men and women have made a personal choice not to marry to legitimise their sexual lives. Some feminists who wish to have children in conditions of their own choice have succeeded in establishing themselves and their children in communal networks of friendship and moral support. Opinion is divided between those who do and those who do not believe that these groups should be financed by public funds, i.e., by taxes collected from others who work to provide themselves and their families with everyday needs. There is probably no logical answer that would satisfy all sides of what has become a political argument. Feminists continue to point out that women remain disadvantaged in waged work and are still shouldering unequal burdens of domestic work. They claim that, irrespective of whether women are working, most of them continue to do 80 per cent of domestic chores. A recent book *What is to be done about the family?** which gives information about the social and political issues of the day, states:

> We want neither to prescribe nor to prevent traditional family arrangements, but to increase the possibility of choice and equality in our domestic lives (though we are totally opposed to the legal terms of marriage which define women as dependent). We want benefits and policies which provide a genuine supportive framework in which we can go about raising our children and caring for dependent people. We want to give value to the sorts of work women have always done. But we want to do it differently, in ways that allow a greater choice for both men and women. Feminists want a society where there is real opportunity between women and men, where both can and must assume greater control over domestic life and support those in need of care.

The development of family planning services has been one of the biggest steps forward this century in changing women's status, and it has sometimes provided better lives for the children of smaller families. † Child

---

*Edited by Lynne Segal. Penguin, 1983.

† In 1930 five separate organisations united to form The National Birth Council; in 1939 the Council changed its name to The Family Planning Association and had already established 65 family planning clinics.

allowances and social security benefits have gone a long way to improving family budgets. Legal abortion has become far more available on widely interpreted medical grounds.

Relationships under stress within any kind of family structure have caused some children to react – sometimes violently –against what they see as personal deprivation and impossible conflict surrounding them. There is a growing belief that the worst threat to the well-being of children and their good health is the gradual reduction of their growing-up years. Much too soon, it seems, children regard themselves as adults. 'Child Liberators' have demanded political franchise, minimum rates of pocket money, sexual relations and even protection from parental control. They claim that children mature quicker these days, but there is little evidence that maturity is taking place earlier even though there is a slightly earlier menarche and commencement of physical development for some girls. A minority of under-sixteens may be mature for their years in a world that seems to have presided over the general lowering of the standards of child behaviour.

Over the past three decades alcohol dependence, glue sniffing, under-age sexual activity and drug-taking have increased. A 1983 report from the Department of Health which was instigated by Action on Smoking and Health (ASH) – an organisation started by the Royal College of Physicians in 1971 – gave the startling revelation that school children were spending £60 million each year on cigarettes. (The law does not allow them to buy cigarettes under the age of sixteen.)

The issue of contraceptives to girls under sixteen – often without proper instruction or health education – has prevented more teenage pregnancies but it has also created a hazardous situation for some who have become sexually active before they have had a chance to develop a sense of responsibility for themselves and those around them; and there has been an increase in sexually transmitted diseases.

If the family has lost its hold and influence on young people who grow up 'too fast', then television is often blamed for its concentration on popular and violent programmes which might encourage them to mimic the good-looking 'criminals' they see on the screen. Some, indeed, seem to have lost all sense of feeling or respect for older people. Old men and women – even babies – have been brutally attacked and robbed. Such behaviour is attributed to hooligans and vandals, but the public's seeming disregard of these activities helps to increase the problems these young people are causing while publicity tends to make them feel more important in their acts of crime.

Charles Dickens and Charles Kingsley used to make their contemporaries aware of the horrors of child-hanging and imprisonment and child-labour in factories and chimneys in a world where child mortality was high. Many young parents nowadays do their best to protect their children from the dangers of the adult world – at least for the first sixteen years of their lives – in the belief that the erosion of childhood brings about many unfortunate consequences; but unless there is more guidance and support for them, young children may lose their way and fail to integrate properly into society.

CHAPTER II

Women and doctors

The first ten years of my work for Women's Health Concern convinced me that I was still struggling in that area of traditional ignorance and neglect that I had discovered years previously. Many women, throughout the world, were still suffering from health problems for which remedies were now available but which they failed to obtain. The full extent of this discrepancy was unknown but our experience at WHC left no doubt that it was of great proportions.

WHC counselling courses and symposia

People's thirst for knowledge of modern medical treatments, and the support of the work Women's Health Concern was doing by doctors and nurses, became apparent through those who attended the WHC counselling courses, and the two symposia on 'The Health of Women at Work'. The reaction by occupational health nurses who work in surgeries in large organisations showed that we were filling a real need:

> The WHC courses we attended have helped us to understand the symptoms and the possible extent of suffering of the women themselves and those around them. Before this we had little knowledge of these illnesses. We are pleased to have first-hand information about the treatments available and the possible benefits and hazards. We think counselling courses should be included in nurses' training.

A psychiatric nurse who attended a study-day for nurses at the Chelsea Hospital for Women in London wrote:

> I have long since recognised that many women are admitted to the acute units of psychiatric hospitals either premenstrually or during the first few days of menstruation and that behaviour, suicidal feelings and/or the experience of hallucinations and delusions disappear spontaneously after a few days.

Typical of many women was the wife of a doctor who was suffering from PMS following the birth of two children. She asked WHC for advice and help to find appropriate medical treatment. It is not unusual for doctors' wives to be neglected by their husbands who are too busy with all kinds of ill patients. In this particular instance the doctor attended one of the WHC counselling courses and expressed his appreciation of the treatment his wife had received from the specialist team who were treating PMS sufferers at St Thomas' Hospital. A year later his wife had learned to cope with her problems and had almost forgotten her previous dilemma.

But although we were by now helping thousands of individual women to obtain appropriate treatment for their different health conditions, it was clear that many were still left to suffer, perhaps in silence, or at the hands of doctors who still felt that women's cyclic health problems would go away if they were left alone. Some doctors, however, were willing in principle to refer women to available clinics for proper medical assessment by consultants. Throughout the world such facilities are scarce, but where they do exist they are providing an invaluable service. In Britain medical ethics have established the custom that doctors provide patients with referral letters to the specialists. This enables important aspects of the medical history or treatment to be communicated to the specialist and is clearly in the interests of the patient. Some doctors are meticulously correct about this and write detailed and helpful letters. However Dr Mansel Aylward – WHC's medical adviser in Wales – wrote as follows in the WHC Annual Report 1982–3:

> Of the hundreds of patients referred to our Endocrine, Rheumatology and PMS/Mastodynia clinics we can only hope to see a small proportion of the whole and must therefore rely heavily on the quality of information supplied by the medical practitioners in their referral letters. It is regrettable to report that only a small number of referral letters provide sufficient information upon which to base an appraisal of the nature and/or urgency of the problem.

It is also the case that, because of shyness and lack of articulation when talking to their doctors, many women are unable to discuss their conditions fully and clearly. Many fail to mention problems like painful sexual intercourse which is a common difficulty suffered by middle-aged women. WHC counsellors encourage them to overcome this diffidence and to speak frankly – whether their doctors are men or women. Some –but by no means all – women express a strong preference for women doctors but, in view of the shortage of good doctors of either sex who have training and the inclination to treat women's problems properly, this attitude is seldom helpful. Doctors are all trained in the same way and, indeed, some of the most unsympathetic of them are women. Of course, everyone has the right to express a personal preference; indeed, some women express a preference for good men doctors. Many unfortunate women, due to traditional customs, are barred from seeing any doctors at all unless they can be attended by a woman doctor. As the years go on one hopes there will be more women doctors who will be prepared to take further studies necessary for them to become gynaecologists and endocrinologists. They will then be as valuable as are the present specialists in this field.

Seeking a second opinion

In Britain NHS patients, women included, are entitled to seek a second opinion from a consultant specialist in a national health clinic and no prudent GP refuses – which is not to say that all readily accede to such requests. Doctors alone have the responsibility of deciding on the treatment which they prescribe and they are entitled to decline suggested treatments if they consider them to be unsuitable. Women have the right to change their doctors if they feel they are not being treated properly, but this can be difficult, and sometimes impossible if doctors' lists are full or if other doctors are not available in their districts.

Nurse-counsellors and psychotherapists

Many doctors have asked WHC where they might refer women to specialist clinics and medical consultants and, in particular, they have asked about the possible facilities for general counselling and psychotherapy sessions. I have always believed that professionally trained nurses are the people who make the best counsellors and that nurse-counsellors could relieve many of the problems that are caused by lack of good communication between doctors and patients. Cooperation between doctors and counsellors could benefit patients, ensure adequate medical supervision and ease the doctors' workload. Provided they are given the support of doctors and are trained to be counsellors many nurses would welcome the responsibilities entailed in the management of women's health problems. They would take histories, advise patients to keep monthly charts, assist in supervising treatment, and help to advise women about their basic health and personal problems. This work is becoming increasingly important in large organisations where female staff work more efficiently when their common health disturbances are recognised and dealt with by industrial doctors and nurses.

From the beginning, the essence of WHC's work has necessitated counselling at all levels. It started with telephone calls from women asking for advice, as well as letters. In the early 1980s women were still travelling great distances to talk to someone who was able to give them specific information and advice. We also try to help women who might benefit from psychotherapy and the deeper analysis it involves and we have had some encouraging response. But, not always. Some women decide not to continue with this type of therapy and unless the woman herself is able to seek talking-treatment and realises her need for doing so, her family, friends and workmates will become sufferers too. Many husbands, friends, sons and daughters have asked us what they can do to improve things for themselves as well as the women they want to help. It is not easy; there are no ready answers. Someone with knowledge and understanding, who can listen for about half-an-hour to a distressed woman who wants to talk about her personal worries, has to ask the key question – What is it that is troubling you most? This often enables a good counsellor to decide how best to try to find the right type of help for her.

Unfortunately it is not possible for everyone to be helped – either by medical treatment or by counselling and, sadly, there are many who are unable to help themselves. Many refuse to see doctors and, if they do see them, they often expect some immediate miracle relief for problems that may be only psychological. Also some women do behave in a manner impossible to deal with. One doctor, writing in the weekly magazine *Doctor* in 1983, described one experience with a woman patient.

'She needed lengthy counselling but insisted on returning home . . . when I called the next morning I spent time getting a lengthy social history . . . she had been abandoned by her family and her two children had been taken into care because of her uncontrollable epilepsy . . . her husband had behaved abominably and life did not seem worth living without her children . . . I never met her husband, and the social services department – in the unfeeling way they have – seemed unlikely ever to relinquish the children who meant so much to her . . . the next few weeks were even more shattering. Her frequent fits could not be controlled by medication . . . She eventually took a small cry-for-help size overdose in her distress . . . I wasn't sure why she did this because we were all doing our best to answer her frequent cries for help – me, my partners, the deputising service, the social services department, the psychiatrist, Samaritans, neurologists and the 70-year-old neighbour who felt so sorry for her that she did the housework and shopping and provided nourishing meals . . .

Then her notes arrived from the Family Practitioners' Committee (FPC) and I must say it was a revelation to me that her many previous doctors should write such things about a patient . . . The Social Services Department's report was even worse . . . it said that she was immature, unable to make personal relationships and inadequate . . . she had repeatedly beaten her children and two husbands had fled, one with a fractured skull . . . She was known to psychiatric units usually after taking a small overdose and discharged herself . . .

I had signed her medical card before I read these reports and cannot agree with all of them . . . Anyone who can bypass a long waiting list and walk into a three-bedroom council house, have rent paid and get every allowance you've heard of – and some you haven't – from the DHSS and have shopping, housework and cooking done by a neighbour is not inadequate . . . She can get a visit from any of us at any hour by either having a bad fit and falling into the fire or by feeling

compelled to take an overdose, cut her wrists or jump into the canal . . .
I've met enough men in her house to make me doubt that she's unable to
make relationships and she expressed herself forcibly to her husbands
and children . . . Whether her fits are uncontrolled because she doesn't
take her tablets or because she is not an epileptic I have yet to decide. But
I have decided the next time she rings me during the night and is about to
jump into a canal I shall advise her to find a deep place . . .

It is important, however, not to let problems grow out of proportion.
For the most part the women who have turned to WHC for expert advice
have been genuine health sufferers. Some have been dangerously ill by the
time they found us, but have responded to the treatment offered by our
medical advisers and colleagues. Several of them had been waiting too long
for hysterectomy operations and were suffering heavy and sometimes
almost continuous bleeding because of fibroids (non-cancerous lumps in
the womb). They needed urgent medical attention, but somehow their
own doctors had failed to know about this and they were being left on long
hospital waiting lists for operations. Lack of communication between these
women and their doctors was sometimes to blame, but there has never
been any resentment on the part of doctors when their patients managed to
have themselves referred to specialists quickly through our liaison with
them and their doctors. On the contrary, everyone concerned seems to
have been satisfied with the outcome.

Human relations play an enormous part in this, but the moral we
should all learn is that there is need for the right kind of health education
for our children of today who will have to become more and more
responsible for themselves in the future. Some persistent and outdated
attitudes will have to change so that all doctors will recognise and treat the
problems of individuals who seek their advice. A good doctor has always
taken into account the relevant factors – which include heredity,
upbringing, socio-economic circumstances and previous medical history
–and has then prescribed a treatment of proven efficacy, if one has existed.
If not, the doctor has to decide how best to deal with each situation,
knowing that no single treatment is suitable for everyone.

A 1981 survey on medical care by the Institute of Social Studies found
that 90 per cent of patients were satisfied with the care they received from
their GPs but that there were also some well-founded complaints. These
include:

(a) *Waiting too long to see doctors* and *Difficulties in getting
appointments*. Sometimes you are asked to wait several days and if you
need to see a doctor urgently you have to make a fuss to get immediate
attention. It may be difficult to get past the receptionist, yet it is only by
speaking to the doctor that satisfaction can be had. Doctors' terms of
service require that patients' health should not be put at risk by having to
wait for appointments.

(b) *Problems with receptionists.* Receptionists can be curt and act as if they are doing you a favour rather than providing a service. They sometimes try to prevent the doctors from seeing you, occasionally give unprofessional advice, and have been known even to provide prescriptions (which is illegal).

(c) *Lack of confidence in the General Practitioner (GP).* Sometimes you feel that your busy GP has no time to talk to you. The GP may not give adequate information unless you ask the questions to which you need answers.

(d) *Feeling rushed.* You may have to wait half-an-hour or more to see your GP, then it can take him about two minutes to write a prescription even before you have had time to explain your problems properly.

(e) *Inconvenient hours.* Surgery hours often match working hours and surgeries are usually shut at weekends except for a short time allocated to emergencies on Saturday mornings.

In doctors' surgeries it seems, there can often be a woeful lack of trained supportive assistance, and social conscience is sometimes in short supply.

The medical and nursing professions in Britain have been faced with much criticism regarding the systems that envelop them. The demands on general practice, the fundamental element of primary care, have increased beyond reasonable hopes that it could provide satisfactory patient care for everyone who seeks it. The need for changes in the NHS has become clear but cash limitations imposed by the government on local medical health authorities have resulted in the closure of certain hospitals and medical and other facilities. Posts have been left vacant and restrictions have been imposed on travel and study leave. Crippling strikes in hospitals over pay, with enforced involvement for everyone employed in them, have left bad scars and nurses have had to make overtly clear their professional identity and expectations in a society that seemed to ignore the skills they had worked to achieve in their years of training. Cries for 'more money or else' have been a nightmare for those who still have a sense of caring for the sick as the basic reason for being a doctor or a nurse.

Pressure groups

The Patients' Association was formed in 1963 precisely to deal with complaints presented by people who consider they have suffered mis-handling of their health problems.

On a wider scale and under a 'no politics and no religion banner', the traditional women's movements such as the National Federation of Women's Institutes (NFWI), have done good by informing successive governments, over many years, about the well-researched resolutions passed by their members. To give one example, the WIs effective 'Keep Britain Tidy' campaign, started by members in Northumberland in 1954, was given a financial grant in 1958 by the government to help progress their initiative in helping Britain to achieve a cleaner and healthier environment.

Another pressure group, trying to isolate what it considered to be abuses in the health services and to promote patients' rights, was given a grant of £37,000 by The Greater London Council (GLC) to cover its work for at least one year. It aimed to create a scheme whereby patients could report side-effects of the drugs they were taking. They complained that the yellow-card-system, in which only doctors can report problems with drugs, was inadequate. A spokesman for the General Medical Services Committee (GMSC) was reported as saying he had doubts whether the ideas of this particular group could work, as information based upon what patients feel about the side-effects of drugs could be of questionable value. He felt that doctors' reports about side-effects were more scientifically credible and that the system could lead to complaints about imaginary side-effects. The same group is producing booklets on health rights in maternity care, the complaints procedure of the National Health Service, and a guide to organisations involved in community care. It feels that when patients, especially women, complain about their doctors they have to have a tight case and it believes they can help them with this.

In America the National Women's Health Network asked the Federal Drugs Administration (FDA) to order a company to recall a certain type of contraceptive intra-uterine device (IUD) known as the Dalkon Shield which it had been sending abroad.* This device had not been used in the USA since 1974 and the group claimed that the makers had shipped 4.7 million of them to fifty-five countries. The Department of Health and Human Services had warned American women still using it to contact their doctors. A government study showed that women wearing this type of device had five times the incidence of pelvic inflammatory disease than women using other types.

When to see a doctor and when to help yourself
Recent reports from the USA have suggested that, because of what many people consider to be unsatisfactory services from doctors, there is a growing agitation for a new kind of health-care system in which doctors would play a more limited but a more exacting role. Some studies have suggested that at least 200 million encounters with doctors have been a waste of time and a doctor from the Medical College of Virginia was reported to have stated that 70 per cent of visits to doctors were unnecessary. In such a situation there is sure to be a boom in the sale of self-help health care kits – but people have kept first-aid kits for emergency use in their homes for years. These have usually included bandages, dressings, a blanket, ointments and tablets like aspirin and thermometers. Those suffering from certain diseases – diabetes for instance – have done their

*The IUD is widely used and many women have no problems with it but some doctors have pointed out that it can be the cause of bacteria entering the uterus and causing infection in certain women.

own tests and have managed their daily treatments carefully but, of course, under medical supervision. It is also possible now to use one of the new self-pregnancy test kits to find out if one is pregnant, for they offer quick and reliable results. There is also a midwife kit that contains what are described as 'the necessary items for uncomplicated deliveries' – this could be useful in an emergency but, for good reasons, it is otherwise illegal for home-births to be carried out by anyone who is not trained as a midwife or a doctor. Some of the kits that are being sold are seemingly unsuitable for practical purposes, however, and the claims made for their possible use by untrained people are beyond the limits of safety.

Some people who are said to have a strong desire to keep away from doctors are, perhaps, now learning to take better care of themselves, and perhaps too they are beginning to understand why and when they should see a doctor. It is analogous to going to a lawyer but wasting money on a matter that does not require the services of a professional legal practitioner.

Many people, however, feel that the reasons for their visits to doctors are ignored or neglected. One of the misunderstandings involved – especially with women – is that some of the problems they suffer from may not relate to any medical cause and often arise because of social and personal difficulties. This is one possible explanation for the over-prescribing of tranquillizers, or the referrals to psychiatrists which is not generally what women expect to hear from their doctors. Sometimes there are legitimate reasons for complaint against doctors who make a wrong diagnosis and then prescribe what specialists consider to be wrong treatments with bad effect; but finding a suitable clinic or a consultant to deal with each person's particular complaint is not always easy. Dr Helen McEwan, who is a consultant gynaecologist in the Royal Infirmary in Glasgow and is also WHC's medical adviser in Scotland, made this comment in the WHC Annual Report 1982–3:

> Women continue to be referred by Women's Health Concern from all over Scotland, in particular from remote parts of the country at some distance from specialist units. They present a wide variety of problems, but the most common referrals are women who consider themselves to be suffering from the premenstrual syndrome. Many of these women fail to respond to medical treatment. Counselling by doctors and nurses, on the other hand, has been found to be helpful and rewarding for many of them.

GPs and deputy doctors

In Britain General Practitioners are employed by Family Practitioners' Committees (FPCs) as independent contractors to provide general medical services for those who register themselves as patients on their lists. They are paid according to the numbers on their lists with extra payments for certain additional items. Most of them keep fairly strictly to their hours and this restricts the number of patients they can see, usually by appointment, in their surgeries from Mondays to Fridays or by selected home visits to those who are considered to be too ill or too old to visit their surgeries. Most people prefer to see the doctor they know, or one of the other doctors working in the same practice, especially in an emergency, but doctors, like everyone else, are entitled to leisure time and two out of every five doctors use deputising services. While the vast majority of calls to these services are dealt with satisfactorily there are legitimate complaints from anxious people when doctors fail to respond quickly enough to emergency night calls. In some cases, not enough deputy doctors have been employed to deal with the large number of calls received in densely populated areas.

The ways in which some doctors have in recent years been dealing with patients has been a far cry from the more personalised relations that often existed in the pre-NHS era. Then, many doctors worked all hours –sometimes to the detriment of their own health – to see every patient who came to their surgeries whether they were panel patients or those who paid private fees. Our ancestors would have been enraged or saddened by some of the things that happen today – for instance, induced labour to ensure that a doctor can have a free weekend.

The medical advances of recent years should surely have improved the situation for peoples' health. They certainly have generally, but only in those cases when the approved treatments are prescribed by doctors for those who will take them properly and who have, of course, managed to obtain the right medical attention for the conditions from which they are suffering.

CHAPTER III

Publicity and a pill scare

All communication to the public about medical matters should be properly informed and soundly presented. Admittedly it requires exceptional skill and talent to communicate the scientific truth on medical matters in a clear and effective way, but, if a film or book, an article or broadcast puts over the wrong message, untold damage can be done.

In July 1983 Dr Michael O'Donnell, an outstanding medical journalist, referred in an article in *Vogue* magazine to a certain BBC Panorama programme in 1981 and the condemnation of it by members of the medical profession who claimed it had got its facts wrong:

> When the arguments were later thrashed out in the scientific journals, it became clear that the arguments used by some of Panorama's experts were less impressive under scientific scrutiny. More significantly, one of the experts withdrew the most telling piece of 'evidence' he had used; but no one outside the medical journals knew of his recantation . . .
>
> Superficial uninformed writing about medicine tends to create an image of a medical Establishment – conservative, purblind, unreceptive to new ideas – surrounded by an Alternative Fringe that is alive with exciting discoveries that include cures for cancer, arthritis, even old age – all the things that the fuddy-duddy establishment has failed to cure because its mind is closed to new possibilities . . .
>
> What is uniting the medical profession in the last quarter of this century is the realisation that further advances will come only if each new treatment is subjected to thorough scientific assessment . . .
>
> Those of us who write about medical advances need to become as self-critical as the best doctors already are. Certainly, we have a responsibility to criticise unthinking orthodoxy and to expose fraud, but we also have a responsibility not to raise false hopes and not to publicise inadequately tested 'cures' or breaksthrough.

The communication channels often seem to have gone out of their way to promote alternative methods purporting to show that members of the public are increasingly attracted to these approaches in preference to orthodox scientific medicine. While it is generally accepted that some homoeopathic remedies: acupuncture, osteopathy, faith healing, hypnosis and relaxation techniques – properly prescribed and applied – can benefit certain people, the wide promotion of new theories, and sometimes the resulting products that have appeared in health shops and elsewhere, have misled many people – who either ignore or know little of how, by the 1980s, orthodox scientific medicine has markedly improved the state of public health. Sometimes it seems that, because people encounter difficulties in obtaining what they consider would be effective medical treatment for their ills – especially if they feel their own doctors are to blame for this – they appear to turn to almost *anyone* or *anything* they have heard about which they think might help them. However in 1983, the British Medical Association (BMA) set up a working party to look into all forms of alternative or 'complementary' medicine.

Many women who have failed to obtain the kind of help they expect to get from their doctors or another reliable source turn to 'agony' columns, partly out of interest, partly in the hope that they will learn something new to help them with their particular worries. If they are ill a good 'agony auntie' usually advises them to see a doctor after she has tried to cheer them up with a few useful hints. This will help some women but most of them read the columns and the letters and answers because they feel their problems might be related to one of the situations mentioned.

Journalists and commentators, as Dr O'Donnell says, have the constant responsibility for not reporting incompletely or simplistically – for example, by isolating one item in a large field of scientific studies and creating thereby emotional and sensational copy of that subject. Such coverage can never be entirely set straight even by the better informed factual articles and broadcasts that may follow.

Pill scare

Unfortunately this was what happened in October 1983 when headlines and street posters suddenly announced 'Cancer and the Pill'. This news item was based on the publication in the 22 October issue of *The Lancet* of two papers associating the use of oral contraceptive pills with an increase of cancer of the breast and cervix (womb). One paper referred to work carried out by Dr Malcolm Pike, newly appointed Director of the Imperial Cancer Research Fund, and his colleagues, while the other paper came from Professor Martin Vessey and colleagues at the Radcliffe Infirmary, Oxford. Dr Pike's work asserted, from studies of 314 breast cancer sufferers compared with the same number of healthy women, that the use of high-level progestogen contraceptive pills before the age of twenty-five 'significantly increases' the risk of developing the disease. Professor Vessey's work involved 7,000 women who were 'on the pill' compared with 3,000 using IUDs. It found thirteen cases of cervical cancer among the former and none among the latter.

The vast amount of medical research that has been done on the pill (and the use of all other medically prescribed drugs) has forever emphasised that no one piece of research is conclusive on its own and a number of well known retrospective studies using the pill has shown that women who have taken oestrogens and progestogens have in fact been protected against developing certain forms of cancer which have been less prevelent than in those not taking this type of treatment.

Dr Gerald Swyer, the WHC Chairman and a senior endocrinologist, wanted – like everyone else who is genuinely involved in the progress of women's health care – to ease some of the problems that had been created both for the millions of worried women and for the doctors they would be seeing. His first letter about the two papers to *The Lancet* was published in their next edition 29 October. He contributed articles to a number of medical journals and took part in several radio programmes. Dr Swyer, in his article published in *The British Journal of Sexual Medicine** referred to eleven important scientific papers that had been published about the use of the pill.

Because Pike et al produced a table of progestogen potencies of various contraceptive formulation, of which they believed the more 'potent' to be associated with greater risks for breast cancer, we were faced with the intolerable situation of the weekend newspapers arrogating to themselves the competence to advise on 'safe' and 'unsafe' brands of pills, to the destruction no doubt of many doctor-patient relationships and to the creation of widespread alarm and anxiety among women. How many unwanted pregnancies will follow the abandonment of oral contraception for other less effective methods is a matter for conjecture but one can be sure they will be considerable and the associated morbidity itself is not insignificant. To have seized on these two papers because they suggest hazards associated with oral contraceptive use, and to give them the publicity they have received, is to overlook the vast and growing literature on the actual and potential effects of the pill. Information on cancer risks is by no means recent but as most of it has been either neutral or favourable, it has received little publicity in the news media generally .

Dr Swyer explained the scientific facts relating to the papers and the reasons why he had strong reservations about the two recent papers and their findings that related to the potency of progestogens. One of the points he made was that inadequate consideration had been made in Professor Vessey's paper of the established connection between the age when girls first start sexual activity and the number of different partners each one has had and the known risks that relate to cervical cancer. This fact has been established for some thirty years.

Dr Swyer was also quoted in an article in the *Daily Telegraph* on 23 October 1983:

*December 1983; Volume 10, No. 103.

It is quite impossible to classify compounds with the amount and kind of progestogens they contain without taking into account several other factors . . . I don't think any of the advice just given out on the risk factors related to different pills is likely to be much use at present.

Dr Swyer said that his own findings in 1982 had been based on the effects of four progestogen mixes with a fixed quantity of oestrogen and they were quite different from some of the progestogen data in Dr Pike's tables.

There were many reports of what other doctors throughout the country had to say. In *Doctor*: Dr Alastair Donald, former council chairman of the Royal College of General Practitioners, described the press reports as causing 'enormous anxiety' and made the point that it was impossible for the public to interpret academic scientific reports in a relevant way and that he felt no way had yet been found to convey scientific information to them without causing panic. He and his partners in their Edinburgh practice were – like practising doctors everywhere else – inundated with inquiries from anxious women. Lord Winstanley, President of the Birth Control Campaign, expressed his concern about a possible setback for world-wide achievements that had been made to start to control the ever-increasing population and he pointed out that if every British pregnancy was a wanted pregnancy at the time of conception, we would never have had a population problem. The point was also made that all doctors know there may be risks with the pill but that pregnancy has its dangers as well. Dr Barbara Thomas, co-ordinator of the DHSS breast-screening study at Guildford in Surrey – which is concerned with retrospective as well as prospective studies being done with large numbers of women – thought that although the data on the two papers looked convincing, there were a lot more factors and many more questions still to be answered. Dr William Styles, honorary secretary of the RCGP, had discussed the reports with other doctors and they all hoped the message would go home to women that they should have regular cervical smear checks. Dr Angela Mills, National Medical Adviser of the Family Planning Association, said 'We feel much of this scare is ill-founded and we are worried it might create a great deal of anxiety among women. We want to reassure them. We know we can prevent cervical cancer if smears are done regularly. If women are worried they should seek advice and if necessary change their form of contraception to something that gives them no anxiety.'

WHC inquirers have long been asking us for advice about how often they should have cervical smears and where they can have them done. The Committee on Gynaecological Cytology of the DHSS has recommended that women should have cervical smear tests as soon as they start to take the pill and again five-yearly at ages 20, 25, 30 and up to age 65. If a woman has reason to believe she needs a cervical smear at any time because she is suffering some problem she has the right to ask her doctor to either do a smear for her or to send her to a clinic where it can be done. In some other countries, including Canada and the USA, a much more aggressive policy of frequent cervical screening has been adopted for some time but an annual Pap (Papanicolau) smear has come in for much criticism.

One important factor for future consideration in Britain will be the provision of more well staffed cervical smear laboratories. In the Manchester area, at the Christie Hospital, Withington, a consultant cytopathologist has pointed out that they are overworked trying to cope with 5,000 smears a week – 1,000 a day – from the north-west of England. Five years ago only one-third of the smears they dealt with came from family doctors and in 1983 70 per cent of them came from General Practitioners. This was good news because it meant that more women were asking their GPs to do smear tests.

Following the furore caused by this particular pill scare we at WHC noticed that some WHC inquirers were reacting more philosophically than they had on previous such occasions. Many of them were able to take a much more balanced view on the known benefits as opposed to the possible risks of taking 'the pill', and they were becoming increasingly aware that low-dose drugs are generally less likely to cause harm. But with the contraceptive pill, the ingredients have to be potent enough to prevent unwanted pregnancies and to maintain regular menstrual cycles.

There were many inquiries also from women taking progestogen treatments for various health problems, all of which could and should have been answered by the doctors and consultants who were treating them. For, in the final analysis, only the women herself can decide whether or not she wishes to take *any* pill, but in making her decision she is entitled to have sound and professional advice.

Sadly, within three months of this pill scare *The Times* of 12 January 1984 reported that hundreds of women in Britain had become unintentionally pregnant. The number of abortions was also increasing and there would be many unwanted babies.

The extent of the damage caused by this particular example of media abuse of health news, it will never be possible to assess. Let readers and viewers always be presented with facts and a balanced picture of whatever subject is being portrayed or discussed. That is not only right in itself; it is also the only basis on which people can look after their own health.

CHAPTER IV

Basic health care and potential hazards

'Take care of yourself' are often the parting words between friends. Yet, in spite of all the publicity for different ideas and theories that inform well women how they can stay that way, many people remain ignorant of simple facts: those relating to personal hygiene, the need to eat the right foods, the avoidance of excessive smoking and alcohol, the importance of sufficient sleep and exercise, and of creating time for leisure interests whenever work and personal commitments permit. All people need to organise a suitable life-style for themselves. Lack of knowledge, or acceptance of that knowledge, can have unpleasant consequences for health and destroy the self-confidence which we need to take proper care of ourselves and to radiate happiness and security.

Nutrition

Let us look at the need for a good diet. Life has become more casual and many people eat more snack food instead of formal meals. These snacks may be low in essential nutrients and, while many people skip meals because of lack of time, others eat too much and grow fat. Many consume too little *fresh* food. Nutrition is a relatively young science which still rests on evidence that is often weak and frequently discounted. At the same time it is generally accepted in western countries that bad nutrition can cause high blood pressure, obesity, heart disease, diabetes and cancer of the bowel. Such problems can usually be avoided.

During the second world war food was rationed in Britain. Government advisers at that time provided a national diet based upon minimum nutritional requirements and they took certain additional measures to improve health. For instance, calcium carbonate was added to the national flour and some experts today believe it was a mistake to have removed it since. Vitamin D was also added to margarine, which helped to reduce rickets. Since then commercial enterprise has taken over, often with 'junk foods' that contain too much sugar and too many additives.

For those who want to eat a healthy balanced diet plus supplements *where necessary* of vitamins, minerals and other essential nutrients – there is an advice leaflet issued by The Health Education Council which explains why we should eat more fibres in our food. It suggests wholemeal bread, potatoes, cereals with wheatgerm and bran, more meals based on beans, peas, lentils and other pulses; and also that we should use meat and eggs more sparingly and eat plenty of salads, fresh vegetables and fresh fruit. (Whenever I lecture and talk about fresh fruit I remember my visits to local African markets which gave me my first opportunity to taste freshly picked little bananas in Tanzania and green oranges in Ghana and Nigeria; after that they never tasted quite so good anywhere else!) But the right kind of foods are readily available nowadays and extras can usually be found in health food shops. It is not necessary, in fact, to spend a lot of extra money to achieve a simple nutritious diet. Indeed, reasonable reduction of the animal protein content (meat, fish, etc.) can keep the cost of healthy meals below that of unhealthy ones.

Many of our eating habits are established by personal taste and choice rather than by instincts – often to our disadvantage. At the WHC medical symposium in April 1983 Dr Richard Petty, a London physician, talked about 'food-induced migraine by additives'. He referred to 'The Chinese Meal Syndrome' which can be caused by an excess of monosodium glutamate used in many popular Chinese dishes, and he also mentioned nitrates that are often used in 'hot dogs'.

Some children have become conditioned to eat junk foods constantly – typical lunches being fatty chips, burgers and ice creams. A number of professional nutritionists emphasise that carbohydrates in fats and sugar can destroy the ability to concentrate, to learn lessons, and to be able to sit still. They also point out that too much junk food can change the levels of blood sugar or glucose in the blood and so cause tension, fatigue, headaches, irritability and anti-social behaviour.

Professor Christopher Nordin, during a talk to members of the press in London in May 1983 pointed out how it is widely assumed that malnutrition is a Third-world problem and that there is little scope for nutritional science in Western countries. He said:

> The concept of malnutrition should embrace not only under-nutrition but also bad nutrition, and in this sense malnutrition is probably as widespread in the wealthier countries as in the poor ones. However, whereas there is a solid body of scientific knowledge widely disseminated which comprehends the minimal requirements of deprived populations and can direct nutritional aid accordingly, there is no corresponding corpus of knowledge to determine the nutritional policies of Western countries . . . The bulk of present-day disease is due to a combination of genetic and environmental factors and nutrition is one of the most important of the latter. Evolution has worked by eliminating those people whose genetic strains could not survive their environment and it has done this over a very long period. The environment has now changed so rapidly that evolution cannot adapt quickly enough. Some people can tolerate Western diets. Those who die prematurely are examples of evolution at work before our eyes. The

environment will change again and the painful adaptive process to existing conditions will be wasted. The only solution is to take charge of our own destiny and not wait for evolution to do the work for us. It is surely significant that kidney stones and hip fractures are rare in Third-world countries where animal protein intake is so much lower than in the west. It is reasonably clear that some people tolerate high intakes of fat, salt and animal protein better than others. Non-specific appeals to whole populations to change their dietary habits do not make much impact but screening of individuals to identify people at risk and provision of specific advice to such individuals is a practicable policy given the will and resources. Relatively simple procedures could be devised for this purpose.

Professor Nordin asked a telling question – 'How many individuals are prepared to take the trouble to modify their life-styles now for the sake of a healthier old age?' He appealed to the media, with their enormous influence on public opinion, to play a part and added, 'Death cannot be avoided but there is a lot to be said for working towards a healthier old age'.

Professor Nordin's research work into bone deterioration and fractures in older women at the Mineral Metabolism Unit at the Leeds General Infirmary is continuing now at the Royal Adelaide Hospital. Both Professor Nordin, and Professor Gilbert Gordan at the University of California, have contributed to establishing the need for the use of preventive medicine to halt the development of osteoporosis (thinning of bones), especially for the estimated 25 per cent of women who suffer from it in their later years. They recommend doctors to use long-term therapy with oestrogens and progestogens (for those who can benefit by it) and increased calcium intake, adequate vitamin D and, where possible, increased exercise.

Smoking abuse
The Causes of Cancer** is the title of a book written by two eminent cancer epidemiologists at the Radcliffe Infirmary in Oxford – Professor Sir Richard Doll and Richard Peto. The book includes background material from a report on cancer to the US Congress which shows that, although cancer is not a modern disease, various common types of it are largely avoidable. Life-style and other environmental factors are explained and divided into twelve categories: tobacco, alcohol, diet, food additives, reproductive and sexual behaviour, occupation, pollution, industrial products, medicines and medical procedures, geophysical factors, infection, and unknown causes.

The book demonstrates the effects of smoking on cancer of the lung – 30

**Oxford University Press, 1982.

per cent of US cancer deaths in 1981 were due to tobacco – and this situation is expected to continue to increase for some years because of the delayed effects of the adoption of cigarettes on earlier decades. The authors believe it is possible that some nutritional factors may eventually be found which will be of comparable importance to the menace of smoking.

But in spite of such information and publicity against the dangers of smoking, many people continue to smoke. They perhaps believe 'it will never happen to me'. Women who smoke when they are pregnant, however, not only harm themselves but they risk the infliction of unpleasant health hazards on their babies and they probably influence their children – perhaps as young as ten or eleven years to smoke too.

Doctors are constantly urging their patients not to smoke. The BMA, the RCGP and ASH have blamed successive governments in Britain for the failure of education programmes on the subject and they claim that both Labour and Conservative administrations have persistently refused to back their efforts to reduce smoking with larger, more specific warnings on cigarette packets and restrictions on advertising. A spokesman from the BMA was reported to have said: 'All the evidence proving that smoking does damage health is only worthwhile if it is backed by proper restrictions, yet the government has consistently refused to intervene'.

There have been a number of surveys that study smoking attitudes and behaviour. The medical authorities were dismayed by recent findings that more than half of the people questioned still believed smoking does not damage their health. This particular three-year study was conducted by the Office of Population, Censuses and Surveys (OPCS) for the DHSS. They questioned 3,764 smokers and non-smokers. Their conclusions showed widespread support for anti-smoking measures, including the raising of the legal age for buying cigarettes and the banning of smoking in public places. Many of them had been made aware of the tar yield in different brands of cigarettes – 85 per cent used tipped cigarettes and more than 90 per cent used low-tar brands. Half of them said they had not found it hard to stop smoking and only six per cent of these said they had put on weight or felt ill-tempered as a result. However FOREST – the Freedom Organisation for the Right to Enjoy Smoking Tobacco – rejected the OPCS findings as 'biased and unreliable'. It cited other surveys, conducted by Market & Opinion Research International (MORI) and the National Opinion Poll (NOP), which had shown that most people believe they should be free to choose whether they smoked or not. Personal freedom to do the things we want to do that will not harm others is one thing; but if we are harming ourselves without being told fully of the possible hazards that is quite another.

Alcohol abuse

Because of the steep rise the world over in the occurrence of alcohol-related diseases The Conference of Medical Royal Colleges and their faculties, including the Royal College of Physicians established an organisation in Britain in 1983 called Action on Alcohol Abuse (AAA). This emphasised that the campaign was not against the reasonable use of alcohol but against its abuse; and it seeks strict curbs on advertising and the promotion of drinks, rigorous enforcement of drink-drive laws, more cash for research and treatment and a government programme to reduce drink problems. It aims to boost prevention rather than cure, because, as its chairman, Professor John Strong, says, there is no doubt that, whatever treatment is offered to casualties of alcohol abuse in whatever hospital, only one-third get better, one-third go their own way and one-third deteriorate. Alcohol intoxication has been involved in causing the deaths of more than 500 young people each year in Britain as well as 80 per cent of deaths from fire, 65 per cent of serious head injuries, more than half the homicides, 40 per cent of traffic accidents involving pedestrians, 35 per cent of fatal accidents and a third of domestic accidents. Since the early 1970s deaths from cirrhosis of the liver have risen by 63 per cent and heavy drinkers have a forty-times-greater risk of developing cancer of the upper respiratory tract. The cost of treating a victim of alcohol abuse in hospital can be between £700 and £1,400 per week.

The road to recovery for most alcoholics is never simple. The long-standing and successful work of the international movement Alcoholics Anonymous (AA) was started in USA in 1935 and spread to many other countries. It came to Britain in 1947. It is an outstanding example of one great self-help success and is self-supported in every way by its members who have all suffered from alcohol problems and have made their way individually to AA for help and advice. It has enabled them to keep their secrets which, incidentally, is an important factor to people who want to find the right source of help.

Treatment and care for alcohol and drug abusers

Most clinics, and specialist clinics which treat alcohol and drug abusers, are there to give support in the form of counselling and substitute drugs. Most sufferers need their lives to be taken over for a period of time by patient, responsible and caring people whom they can learn to trust. They have to restore, at least in part, the self-confidence and dignity they have lost. Doctors need to decide whether addiction to alcohol and drugs is a primary illness or a reaction to outside pressures. As for every illness, it is no good treating the symptoms unless the underlying cause is discovered and dealt with, otherwise the symptoms will return. There is no doubt that greater and earlier doctor-involvement with addicts could help in identifying them and treating them. Community work by members of alcohol teams has frequently enabled doctors to treat addicts themselves instead of sending them to hospitals. Doctors are, after all, ideally placed not only to treat them but also to deal with any accompanying family tensions.

43

Potential hazards for women

The number of women and young people who have become dependent on narcotics, and a wide-ranging number of other drugs, has increased alarmingly in recent years. In December 1982 the Advisory Council on the Misuse of Drugs estimated that there were 40,000 people in this category in the United Kingdom. The National Council on Alcoholism put the number of alcoholics in the thousands – and thousands more have a drink problem. For women, there are special potential health hazards for those who smoke and drink to excess and those who are overweight. *Menstrual pain* is more common among smokers. The nicotine in cigarettes dilates blood vessels and increases muscle activity in the uterus (womb) and other organs. Women taking the contraceptive pill are advised not to smoke because of the increased risk (about four-fold) of *thrombosis* (clotting of blood within a vessel). Overweight also increases the thrombosis risks.

If surgery is contemplated, consideration should be given to stopping smoking altogether and to trying to reduce weight before the operation. Most women are aware how alcohol may induce some pain relief but excessive drinking causes extensive physical and mental deterioration at any age and women are more susceptible to this than men due to a difference between the sexes in liver function. Too much drinking also brings about sexual dissatisfaction, and anyone who has had to exist or work with people who have also suffered brain damage through drinking knows how that creates chaos and misery wherever it is found.

CHAPTER V

Well women and ill women –
self-help and existing facilities

In an ideal world – whether in good health or when ill – most women would observe the basic rules of health care, would apply the reliable methods of self-help and know when, where and how to seek further help if it were needed. They would no longer be obsessed with many of the worries they have brought upon themselves. Their horizons could be wider because they would be able to do more of the things they want to do. Their health care would be second-nature to them because they would be rather like good car drivers who look after their cars properly and watch out for snags. All doctors would be sympathetic and helpful about women's ills and all women would be sensible enough to help their cures.

Unfortunately this is not the health care scene today and this may be partly why so many women are now rallying to a call for well-women clinics to be established throughout the country. Such centres must be properly equipped and medically staffed to provide breast screening, cervical smear tests, blood pressure and urine checks and other preventive procedures for *well women*. Existing facilities are usually run by Regional Health Authorities but they are in short supply. Financial shortages have threatened to close some of the old-established women's hospitals and early diagnostic units, but sometimes they have been saved when there has been a public outcry to keep them going.

Some commercial companies and organisations provide health services for their employees. Doctors have been mainly concerned with treating ill people and are generally unable to give adequate attention to providing preventive medicine to those who might benefit by it.* Private doctors and hospitals, as an alternative to the NHS, have provided some good services but this kind of treatment can be expensive and most people are unable to afford it unless they pay for medical insurance which can help to reduce the costs. This is also a subject of political controversy and it remains to be seen how future governments will try to sort it out. However the services and the financial resources of both the NHS and the private sector should continue to complement each other and, so long as this happens, Britain will remain one of the better places in the world for its care of ill people.

*(As explained in the Conclusion to this book The Royal College of General Practitioners is taking steps to change this situation.)

There seems to have been a lack of communication in certain places where women have not been given details of existing clinics run by local health authorities. It has also become apparent that many people have not understood the structure of the NHS and how best they can use its services.

Some twenty years ago the Women's National Cancer Control Campaign (WNCCC) started to alert women to the need and opportunity of cervical screening facilities in many parts of the country. With the co-operation of the Area Health Authorities (AHAs) they then started to run local publicity campaigns to encourage well women to visit their mobile clinics which were taken to shopping centres, housing estates, workplaces and shops. The WNCCC provided thousands of leaflets and posters and they were helped by members of women's voluntary organisations and by publicity in local papers and in radio programmes. They also held public meetings. But the intermittent provision of mobile screening units to every Regional Health Authority could only offer some preliminary answers to the problem of extending cervical screening services to the widest possible number of women. This is especially the case with those most at risk of developing cervical cancer – the women, in fact, who are often the ones who are least likely to avail themselves of the service.

In 1977 the mortality rates for cervical cancer were still over 2,000 each year in Britain* yet only about three million, out of a potential seventeen million women, availed themselves of cervical smear tests. Young mothers and those visiting family planning clinics received the test automatically –older women often missed out on the facilities provided although many of them had been informed that if they had any bleeding or spotting between periods or after the menopause they should see their doctors. Cervical cancer is the only known cancer that can be prevented, by detection of the earliest stages.

Breast cancer is the largest single killer of middle-aged and older women. One in fifteen women may expect to have breast cancer during their lives. In Britain 12,405 women died from this disease in 1982. In 1975 the figure was 11,630. At that time the cost of mammography for both breasts was about £7 and the capital cost of setting up a unit capable of examining about 7,500 women a year was about £20,000; and, of course, suitable buildings were needed to house it and money to maintain and run it. In Southend, Essex, a group of people, including women and doctors, raised enough money to set up a local breast-screening unit and housed it in good premises. Then, some of the local women continued to voice their opinions about the need for more preventive health care in their district and a local newspaper, the *Evening Echo*, organised a survey in which 246 women claimed to be suffering from a variety of women's health problems, and 67 per cent of them said they were unable to talk freely to their doctors. The local Health Authority then agreed to provide space in local NHS

*DHSS Evidence to the House of Commons Select Committee on Expenditure, looking at 'Preventive Health' 1976–7 session. HMSO 1977.

clinics so that further facilities could be set up. The women hoped that this would lead to the establishment of a well-women clinic, and all the time they were continuing to raise funds for this project. At a time when the government was having to enforce health service cutbacks, the NHS and the people in the community were working together to start up local well-women facilities. Similar efforts were being made in many other districts.

Most existing clinics have been set up by Regional Health Authorities or by a collective effort. Some of them are attached to hospitals or to family planning clinics. Centres that have been in existence for some time include those at Islington in London, Brighton, Brentwood and Manchester. Also in London, the well-known early diagnostic breast screening unit was originally set up in Chelsea for a certain period of time for work being carried out at the Royal Marsden Hospital nearby. It was due to be closed in 1981–2 but there were such protests from the doctors who work in it and from the women who have been able to use it that it has survived, at least for the time being.

The DHSS, on the advice of the Joint Working Group on Breast Cancer Screening, did not set up additional screening services but there are two working groups, at Guildford in Surrey and in Edinburgh, which are advising the Secretary of State on the type of screening trials that might be possible and on the safety and improvement of screening techniques. Some research was carried out at University College Hospital, London and elsewhere to determine if radiographers and nursing staff could be trained to interpret mammograms accurately.

It is easy to obtain breast screening and many other medical check-up procedures in the private sector – two of the organisations that provide these services are The British United Provident Association (BUPA) which has branches all over the country, and the Private Patients' Plan (PPP) Medical Centre.

Marie Stopes House in London runs its own well-woman centre which was started in 1921 when Marie Stopes opened the first full-time family planning clinic in the world. In 1925 she moved her clinic to the house where it has been located ever since. It is run by a registered charity for people of all ages who are looking for expert and sympathetic advice on all aspects of contraception, unwanted pregnancy and on physical and emotional problems which may be sexually based. It provides an informal, confidential and accessible service at minimum prices to those who use it. It also provides pregnancy testing, gives advice and help on PMS, counselling and referral for unwanted pregnancy, vasectomy, female sterilisation and psycho-sexual counselling.

An ideal well-women clinic

The Elizabeth Garrett Anderson Hospital for women, near Euston Station in London, is staffed entirely by women doctors and nurses. It had been threatened with closure for several years before it was reprieved in May

1979 after a public outcry. By 1984 it had not only survived but was continuing its vital work for women's health in a new and much wider role. The government had provided a £2.4 million (inflation-proofed) grant to cover much needed renovations and to include two 20-bed wards, an operating theatre, X-ray and out-patients departments, a day-room and the addition of an Early Diagnostic Unit or well-women clinic. The grant was given, however, on the strict understanding that the balance needed to equip and furnish the new hospital, together with the cost of a day-care service with a second theatre, another bed lift and a day ward should be found from voluntary sources. By the end of 1983 all the money had been raised – at least £500,000. The well-women clinic now provides cervical smear tests, breast screening using the most modern equipment, and other check-up tests and procedures when they are considered to be necessary. Well women do not need to get referral notes from their doctors to attend this clinic but they have to make appointments by telephoning or writing to the hospital. Those who have discovered breast lumps or some other abnormal condition in themselves must go to their doctors and ask to be referred to one of the outpatient clinics at The EGA which deal with gynaecological conditions, family planning, PMS, psychosexual problems, dermatology and – in fact – most of women's specific conditions. All these services in this hospital are provided by the NHS.

Many women want to try to help other women and a number of self-help groups have been formed. They can sometimes give consolation to each other by talking over problems together and they can help well women to find work and new leisure interests. They also encourage ill women to seek advice from recognised organisations and sources of help which, of course, is usually a doctor. Voluntary organisations continue to help people with all kinds of problems and the old-established Citizens' Advice Bureaux can often direct their inquirers to helpful branches within reach of their homes. Lonely women – and there are many of them –sometimes benefit by taking part in activities that are organised by local groups.

Ill-women groups

A number of ill-women groups for those who are suffering specific health problems, have been formed. One of these is the Endometriosis Society, which has become a registered charity, with groups in several places. They issue information about their illness to other women sufferers and they share their personal experiences to try to help themselves and each other, bearing in mind that for each one the experience can be different – and this is a very important point.

Endometriosis is a condition in which fragments of the lining of the womb (endometrium) become detached and re-attached to various places in the pelvis and elsewhere. There they react like the lining of the womb itself to ovarian hormones, bleeding with each period. This is liable to lead painful periods and other troubles. Diagnosis has to be made by a gynaecologist who decides whether the treatment has to be surgical, or with hormones or a combination of the two.

Another endeavour to help fellow sufferers was made by two London women who had been upset by *agoraphobia*. They managed to prepare a survey that was evaluated by the Mental Health Foundation. However, after both of them had recovered from their own problems they decided to return to their other interests. Understandably they wanted to forget the health troubles which had made their own lives so difficult. They had, however, helped themselves by taking a serious interest in the problem they were suffering and they had helped others. Their particular enterprise ended there and, for them, this was a healthy decision.

Self-examination

Self-examination of the breasts is one of the important routines about which all women should learn. The Family Planning Information Service and The Health Education Council in London are two organisations that provide free literature on the subject. Whatever her age, a woman should examine her own breasts once a month to observe whether there have been any changes in contour or symmetry. The best time for a menstruating woman to do this is a few days after her period has finished because at that time her breasts are less likely to be swollen or tender. She has to learn how to feel or palpate her breasts and to look at her nipples to see if one or other or both has become inverted and to squeeze them gently to see if there is any unusual discharge. Any dimpling of the breast skin should be noted and if she discovers this or any lumps in her breasts she should see her doctor. Most breast lumps are not due to cancer and they will either disappear or can be treated. It is always wise to get a medical check-up, however, for it is usually less worrying to know the truth.

Some women are reluctant to touch themselves in the genital area but, if they can manage to do so, they could feel inside their own vaginae by using one or two fingers. Sometimes a little KY Jelly, cold cream or even water on the index and middle fingers helps – especially if she has not done this before. By sweeping her fingers around inside her vagina she will discover that the walls are elasticated and that the far end seems to be closed. If she puts pressure against the roof of the vagina she may feel the urge to pass water. This sensation is often experienced when inserting a tampon and is caused because the bladder which contains the urine is situated above the vagina. There is no need to wear rubber gloves when exploring one's own vagina in this way but the hands should be washed first, of course, and the nails cut short. Most women prefer to do it when they are standing with one foot slightly raised on a stool or cushion but different postures are used according to the individual.

During recent years women's groups have been encouraging women to try to look inside their own vaginae by using a plastic speculum (doctor's instrument). They have suggested that this should be done in groups where they can compare what they see with other women and break down taboos about looking at themselves and at each other. They believe that this helps each one to get to know how the inside of her own vagina looks and to spot any changes that take place.

It is important to get to know ourselves and to try to learn as much as possible about the workings of our bodies by touching, feeling and looking at our various parts; but self-examination of the vagina by using a speculum is not a practice I would recommend – especially to those who do not want to learn how to do it. I am not saying that those who do it are wrong. They are, of course, right to do what they believe is helpful to themselves and perhaps to others, but I am sure they realise that self-examination of the vagina is no substitute for a medical pelvic examination which is urgently necessary for women who have vaginal infections and other problems. However, following inquiries which Women's Health Concern had received from women (and men) who were confused by an item they had seen in a particular television programme, I was prompted to write a letter to the British Medical Journal.*

'On 21 January the programme showed a group of women talking about how to use a speculum for vaginal self-examination. Untrained women cannot interpret what they might see even assuming they succeed in exposing the cervix; they could cause damage to the vagina and cervix, and unless the speculum is sterilised they run the risk of introducing infection. Parenthetically, there is an American film which actually shows a group of women passing a speculum from one to the other without even washing it.'

Exercises

It is important to learn how to breathe properly and to perform exercises that can strengthen muscles and maintain muscle tone throughout the body – without overdoing it. Women must not neglect the pelvic muscles that are situated below the diaphragm and help to support the pelvic organs in place.

These include the lower intestines, the uterus and the bladder. The first thing to do is to contract the muscles around the vagina for a second or two and then release them completely. Repeat these contractions with rhythmic movements whenever you think about it. One way to find out about the kind of movement that is needed is to pass urine and then stop the flow suddenly. These localised contractions can be practised at any time – and no one else need know about it – just after waking up or when sitting or standing. Good control of the pelvic muscles helps to control the

*Vol. 286, 3 March 1983.

urine flow, when necessary; it will also improve sexual intercourse and help in childbirth.*

Masturbation

There must be no question of guilt for women who enjoy self-exploration of any part of their bodies; and one practice that offers pleasure at different times is masturbation. This used to be considered only a man's practice which was done partly to relieve himself of excess seminal fluid, especially when he had no sexual partner. Some women give themselves pleasure by gently stroking the area around the clitoris. Sometimes they cross their legs and exert steady and rhythmic pressure on the whole genital area which may stimulate muscular tension throughout their bodies, resembling the tensions developed in sexual intercourse. Some women also find that various kinds of physical activities – riding horses or climbing trees or ropes – will promote feelings of sexual excitement for them. By self-stimulation of the vagina, clitoris and breast, especially the nipples, women can learn to enjoy and understand some parts of their bodies.

Cosmetic and plastic surgery

One of the areas in which many women have failed to obtain suitable attention is cosmetic and plastic surgery. Some women decide they want to improve their looks and body contours and many want to banish scars and blemishes. Those who have had breast surgery need to know about breast reconstruction.

There have been some serious complaints against bungled operations in this area – it was reported that one woman could not close her eye after a £1,000 operation to remove bags and another woman was left with her abdomen looking like 'tramlines' after a slimming operation. In Britain the General Medical Council (GMC) is not ordinarily concerned with errors in diagnosis unless a doctor's neglect raises questions of serious misconduct, but a revised set of rules was published in the Council's 'blue book' on ethics in 1983. It added – 'The question of serious professional misconduct may also arise from a complaint or information about the conduct of the doctor which suggests that he is endangering the welfare of patients by persisting in independent practice of a branch of medicine in which he does not have the proper knowledge and skill and has not acquired the experience which is necessary'. Patients are, of course, free to consult any doctor but the Council's current ruling is that the specialists who are approached directly should inform the General Practitioner of their findings and recommendations before starting treatment unless the patient

---

*The National Childbirth Trust provides detailed instruction on *Kegel* exercises. This charity was founded in 1956 by a group of mothers who wanted to help others to widen their understanding of the whole experience of pregnancy, birth and early parenthood. It has branches and groups all over the United Kingdom.

does not have a GP or expressly withholds consent for the information to be passed. Some GPs are at a loss to know where to refer their patients for cosmetic surgery but the onus still rests with them to seek out an appropriate surgeon or to refer them to reliable sources of information.

Back pain and possible treatments

Back pain is another problem for which many women seek safe and effective help. Manipulation, not specifically chiropractic, is a post-graduate exercise for doctors. These techniques are a specialised form of treatment and cannot be learnt from books. Osteopathy is a profession that has been accepted by the Professions Supplementary to Medicine (PSM). A good osteopath can be invaluable in helping to relieve some problems involving bones and joints but it is important to find one who is reliably qualified and known to be safe and effective.

Chiropractic practice has been popular in the USA for some years but The British Chiropractors Association (BCA) is a fairly new organisation. It currently has over 150 members who have passed out as chiropractors after a four-year training course. The only recognised training school in Europe is the Anglo-European College of Chiropractic in Bournemouth.

About 50,000 patients in Britain are using chiropractors, yet only 11 per cent of them are referred by General Practitioners. As yet there is no state registration for this type of treatment and it is difficult for a patient to tell the difference between a professional or an unqualified practitioner. Manipulation offered by chiropractors is potentially dangerous unless it is performed by a properly trained practitioner. The BCA condemns chiropractic correspondence courses, which claim to teach the discipline by post, as being totally inadequate even for GPs. Chiropractic is a speciality that is fighting for state registration and the course at the college is being considered by the Council of National Academic Awards (CNAA) which can grant degree status.

Women, in particular, often discover for themselves all kinds of techniques they believe to be helpful for relieving different types of pain. The important point to establish is whether or not the techniques they are seeking are likely to be harmful. Doctors generally refuse to recommend any technique that has not been convered by some published research but, at the same time, they are often willing to suggest methods or techniques they know to be safe and which can be helpful. One example, *The Alexander Technique* for back treatment, has proved itself to be an answer for many people suffering pains in their backs. The Alexander Technique, originated by F. Matthias Alexander in the late nineteenth century, is based on a principle that claims to teach us to unlearn destructive physical habits and help to use our bodies in a healthy way.

The skills of a good physiotherapist are important to those who suffer all kinds of injuries, and aches and pains; and a regular massage is no longer a luxury for women, like myself, who find it helps to strengthen muscles and relieve tension in their bodies.

PART II

Women's health problems

CHAPTER VI

Feminine hygiene

The word hygiene, which comes from Hygeia, the Greek goddess of health, reminds us of the vital connection between health and cleanliness.

In densely populated civilized societies, public hygiene is indispensable for preventing the epidemics which devastated cities in former times. Personal hygiene is the responsibility of everyone of us – to keep our bodies clean, our clothes decently laundered and our own environment free as far as possible from pollution. But when one young woman in her teens complained to Women's Health Concern about unbearable irritation, swelling and soreness in her vagina, a headache, high temperature and feeling very sick, a gynaecologist discovered that she had left a soiled tampon inside her and had then inserted a second tampon. Unfortunately, there was little unusual about her negligence. WHC receives a constant flow of calls from women of all ages with distressing conditions that might have been avoided if they had only been more aware of the need for self-care, and especially of the proper use of sanitary protection.

The Skin and its care

The skin is the body's outer protection against the environment and, if intact, it keeps most germs out. It helps to control the body's temperature mainly through the sweat glands which keep the surface moist to increase cooling of the body. It produces an oily substance from the sebaceous glands to maintain the softness of the outer layers – too much makes the skin greasy and too little makes it dry. The skin continually replaces its outer layers with cells from the deeper layers, whilst those on the surface die and flake away, usually unnoticed.

Good circulation of air is necessary because the skin has to 'breathe' to remain healthy, and problems can develop in the parts of the body where air is excluded – the armpits, the groin, or beneath sagging breasts. So, it is very important that clothing should not be worn so tight as to prevent the free circulation of air to the skin.

Washing

Washing removes the sweat, oil, dead cells, dirt particles from the environment and germs which build up on the skin. In the unwashed, germs on the skin multiply rapidly and produce extremely unpleasant-smelling compounds.

People vary in the extent to which they may become smelly and how often they need to wash, depending upon whether they are fat or thin, tend to sweat easily or otherwise, and upon the kind of work they do. A sensible system is to wash the hands several times a day and always after using the lavatory or before preparing food; the face on waking and before going to bed; and the rest of the body once a day if possible.

When anyone is suffering from a skin disease, a doctor's advice should be sought on how and when to wash the affected areas.

Hot or cold water? Hot water is better for washing but very hot water can harm the skin. Hot water is more effective at removing unwanted skin secretions and it opens the pores to help these secretions to emerge from the deeper layers. Finishing off with cold water closes the pores again and reduces the risk of dirt and germs getting in afterwards.

Soap or no soap? Soap, especially when used with *soft* warm water, is best for removing the greasy skin secretions which hold on to dirt, but some people find that soap can irritate more sensitive areas, such as the face. In these cases a mild, unperfumed soap to which their skins are insensitive has to be found by trial and error or else a cleansing lotion, which is more expensive, can be used.

Make-up also needs to be removed at least once a day and the same principles apply. Soap is fine for this, provided it does not irritate the skin; if it does, a non-irritant cleansing lotion needs to be found.'

Baths or showers? It is all a matter of personal preference. Baths tend to be more popular in colder climates and frequent showering preferred in hot countries. Some people consider that showers are more hgyienic because the running water continuously washes away dirt and germs from the skin whilst bath water gets dirtier the longer you stay in it. Other say that you can wash more effectively in a bath.

Possibly the ideal solution would be a bath, followed by a shower – cold to close the pores – ending with a brisk rub with a slightly coarse towel to stimulate circulation, but not so brisk as to damage the skin.

How often and when a bath or shower should be taken is again a matter of choice depending upon climate, how dirty you are and how you feel. Our ancestors rarely bathed at all, claiming that it was weakening or bad for health. We nowadays know better and many people bathe or shower daily without ill effects and indeed to their benefit.

Cosmetics and the skin

It is important to make sure that cosmetics do not harm the skin. All reputable manufacturers take great care to see that their products do not contain harmful ingredients but, despite this, particularly sensitive skins may react to certain preparations. The solution is to avoid these and stick to those which prove harmless. Generally speaking, unperfumed preparations tend to be least likely to affect sensitive skins. All make-up

57

must be removed daily, otherwise it clogs the pores and for those with sensitive skins, the shorter the time the skin is in contact with make-up, the better.

Suntan

Suntan is currently much admired but excessive sunlight, or more especially ultraviolet rays, whether from the sun itself or from a UV lamp, are bad for the skin. Its effects can be very ageing and it can even cause skin cancer. Skin cancer is far more common in white people living in very sunny climates, such as Australia, South Africa and Southern California, than in those living in northern countries. The pigment (melanin), which develops in the skin on exposure to sunlight, protects against harmful effects of UV light. Its presence in dark-skinned races, normally living in tropical countries, is a genetic adaptation to the sunny environment.

When sunbathing on holiday to achieve that fashionable tan, start with a brief exposure only. Twenty minutes is enough on the first day, increase this time very gradually and always use a good quality sun-tan product. There are a number of reliable sun-screen preparations which, if used conscientiously, can avoid much distress and a ruined holiday. If raw areas develop as a result of sunburn there is the added risk of infection.

Problems of perspiration

Too little. To sweat little, whilst possibly convenient, can cause serious problems in a hot, dry climate. Individuals with this tendency can become overheated and develop prickly heat (miliaria). This develops as an irritating rash; rapid cooling with a cold shower is the best treatment.

Too much. A tendency to perspire excessively (hyperhidrosis) is common and a greater nuisance, as it is less easy to control and a source of embarrassment. It may be caused by disease, such as a fever or an over-active thyroid gland, or anxiety, or it may be a peculiarity of the individual's make-up. The whole body may be affected, or only certain areas such as the palms of the hands, soles of the feet, the face, the armpits, beneath the breasts or in the groin. Constant moisture on the skin can cause cracks or peeling scabs, and the feet are particularly prone to this. Germs –bacteria and yeasts – may grow readily on the warm, moist skin, causing offensive odours and even dermatitis.

Excessive sweating is sometimes difficult to treat. Regular washing with soap and water helps to keep the body clean and the odours at bay, but care has to be taken not to irritate affected skin further. Deodorants and anti-perspirants, many of which are available, are valuable so long as they do not irritate the skin. It can make sense to shave the hair under the armpits, and in the groin if there is a tendency to sweat there too. Relatively light and loose-fitting clothing helps. Overweight people are more likely to sweat excessively and to have skin trouble from it because of deep skinfolds – it provides another incentive to lose weight. Talcum powder is useful under the armpits, beneath the breasts, on the feet and in the groins but, as always, make sure it does not irritate the skin.

As underwear is worn next to the skin, the material it is made from and how it is washed is very important. Cotton is always better than synthetic materials because it is more absorbent and detergents, especially ones with biological additives, can irritate some skins. So a mild, pure laundry soap is better for washing underwear. Tight-fitting underwear can also cause problems. For women, pants which are too tight keep the genital area unduly moist and this encourages the growth of germs, so increasing the risks of infection of the bladder (cystitis) and vagina. From a hygienic point of view, open or French knickers and cami-knickers are preferable to the bikini type. Pants should be changed and washed frequently, usually once a day, but those who sweat a lot or produce a lot of vaginal secretion (which is not necessarily in any way abnormal) may want to change more often. Throw-away paper pants have a lot to recommend them, especially when travelling, except perhaps their cost.

Many women prefer tights to stockings but hygienically they are much less satisfactory, greatly increasing the risk of cystitis and the vaginal infection called Thrush (see page 116). The open gusset type of tights are therefore healthier. Similarly, tight-fitting trousers may be fashionable but there is no doubt that, since women have taken to wearing trousers and tights, genito-urinary tract infections have become far more common.

Skin disorders

It would be out of place in a general chapter on hygiene to make recommendations, other than those already mentioned, to anyone suffering from a skin condition which does not quickly clear up with simple remedies. Medical help must be sought, firstly from your GP and then, if necessary, he will refer you to a dermatologist.

Care of the nails

Frequent use of the nail brush with warm water and soap keeps the nails clean. An orange-wood stick should be used *gently* to clean under the nails and to keep the cuticles pushed back when they have been softened with warm water. The nails should be kept trimmed with nail cutters or scissors and a nail file or emery board. They should be kept to such a length as not to interefere with work. If left too long they are liable to split or break. Nail polish is harmless but nail polish remover can dry out the nail and make it fragile unless it contains oil.

The nails are subject to various diseases so, if you are in any doubt about them, consult your doctor.

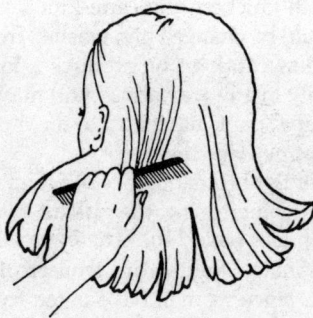

Care of the hair

Regular and frequent brushing and combing is more important to hair care than regular washing and insufficient brushing and combing can lead to dull hair. Frequency of washing depends partly on personal choice and partly on the dryness or oilyness of the scalp. Once a week may be more than necessary for some women and not enough for others but too frequent washing can lead to dry hair. Thorough drying after washing is important. Rinsing in fresh water after sea bathing is essential, otherwise the hair becomes very sticky.

For washing, one of the commercial detergent shampoos can be chosen but a mild soap is perfectly satisfactory if the water is soft. Many medicated brands, designed to combat dandruff, are on the market but some fail to live up to their manufacturer's claims. Brushes and combs should be well washed and dried before each shampoo to help hair remain free from dandruff, and they should never be shared. The use of various kinds of rinses (other than soft water) is really a question of beauty treatment which cannot be considered here. Similarly, the use of hairspray to hold hair in position is not an aspect of hygiene, but it should be borne in mind that its effects are not always harmless to the hair or scalp.

Invasion of the hair with lice is not uncommon, particularly amongst the young, and in some areas it is epidemic. The louse (Pediculus) is an insect which feeds on blood, causing itching and scratching which may lead to other infections. It and its eggs (nits) can easily be seen and destroyed by carefully searching the hair with a nit comb. Ordinary shampoos or soap will not destroy the nits, but one part vinegar diluted with four parts water is said to do so. There are a number of proprietary lotions and shampoos for treating head lice which should be used according to the makers' instructions.

Ringworm, a fungus (Trichophyton), also infects the hair and scalp, and sometimes the nails and skin. Anti-fungal tablets taken by mouth are the only effective treatment but they must be prescribed by a doctor.

Care of the teeth and gums
The best start for healthy teeth is to have been born by a mother whose diet included the necessary vitamins and minerals but no excess of carbohydrate. Proper feeding, with very few sweets as a child, also helps, along with regular visits to the dentist.

Teeth should be brushed with a firm but not too stiff brush, ideally after every meal, but once in the morning and before going to bed is probably more practicable. The choice of tooth-paste – and whether or not it should contain fluoride – is debatable but the importance of a minimal level of fluoride in the drinking water, for the reduction of dental decay, can no longer be seriously disputed.

Brushing should be directed up and down rather than from side to side. This removes most particles of food from between the teeth and helps to keep the gums healthy, but it cannot get rid of all the debris. For this dental floss is highly recommended. Tooth picks can also be used but they are not so effective and should be used with great care in order not to damage the gums.

Bad breath (halitosis) can result from the lodging of food particles between teeth or the teeth and gums. These are decomposed by bacteria in the mouth, producing unpleasant-smelling products which damage the teeth and can lead to infection of the gums (pyorrhoea).

Regular dental hygiene will nearly always prevent bad breath but a mouth wash can be used as an additional precaution. Some highly spiced foods can produce smells which other people may find objectionable. If you do not wish to cause offence, it is best to avoid them unless the rest of the company is also eating them. Smoking also causes a smell which non-smokers in particular find offensive. This is perhaps yet another argument against smoking.

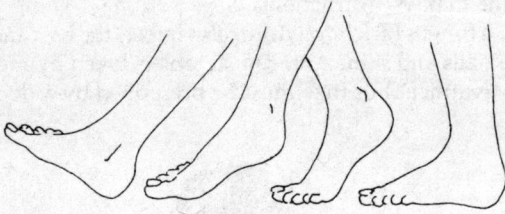

Care of the feet

Properly fitting shoes are essential from birth, to avoid deformities in later life such as bunions and hammer toes. Such problems have to be corrected, sometimes surgically. Shoes should be chosen for comfort rather than fashion.

Hard skin on various parts of the feet, and corns, are the result of badly fitting shoes. Treatment by a chiropodist is necessary. However, unless more sensible shoes are worn, the condition will return. Well-fitting socks or stockings are also important and people whose feet sweat a lot should change their socks or stockings frequently. A dusting powder may also help.

Keeping the toenails well trimmed helps to preserve socks and stockings and prevent in-growing toenails. These can be painful, and medical advice should be sought as the nails may need surgical treatment.

Foot infections, such as athlete's foot and verruca, can be picked up in changing rooms and by dancing or doing gym barefoot. Athlete's foot is a fungal infection (Tinea) between the toes which can be difficult to get rid of. A number of effective fungicidal creams are available from the chemist but if the condition tends to recur, use some of the cream between the toes every day as a preventive. Verruca, the medical name for wart, can make walking very painful. The only satisfactory treatment is surgical removal (curettage) by a doctor or chiropodist.

Care of the genital area

The space between the legs, the perineum, houses three openings to the interior of a woman's body. The front two openings – the urethra, leading from the bladder; and then the vagina, connected to the womb – are enclosed within the vulva or external genital organs. Behind is the anus, the opening of the intestines. Urine passes from the bladder through the urethra, normally excluding germs but sometimes germs do enter and, because the urethra in women is short – much shorter than in men – it is not difficult for germs to reach and infect the bladder, causing cystitis. The vagina always contains germs, but in healthy women these are harmless and tend to keep out others which could be harmful. But because the anus is so near, fecal germs can reach other parts of the perineum and cause infections. It is therefore important – but not so easy – to keep the perineum as clean as possible by regular washing with warm water and after defecation, to wash or wipe *backwards*, away from the vulva.

THE EXTERNAL GENITAL ORGANS

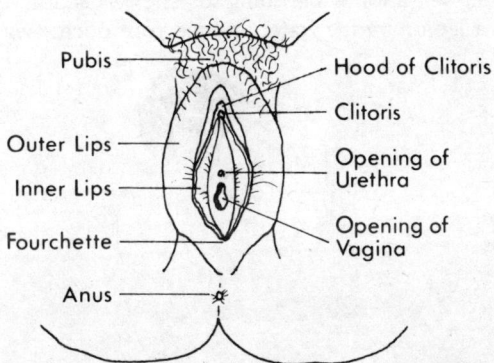

Pubis — Hood of Clitoris
— Clitoris
Outer Lips — Opening of Urethra
Inner Lips —
Fourchette — Opening of Vagina
Anus —

The vagina itself does not need washing – it is self-cleansing – but its secretions which reach the outside must be washed away regularly. The bidet, invented by the French, is unsurpassed for this purpose.

All women produce vaginal secretions and the amount varies not only from woman to woman, but also within a woman's own monthly cycle. Although this is perfectly normal, it can cause embarrassment. For added reassurance and also to preserve underwear, disposable pant-liners can be worn.

Douching. Squirting water into the vagina with some sort of apparatus to clean it is now uncommon and does not generally meet with medical approval. By washing out the normal germs from a healthy vagina you can increase the risk of entry of others, not normally present, which can cause infection. If you regard douching as an important part of feminine hygiene, you should use nothing but plain, warm water (no soap or medication) and *gentle* pressure only.

Infections

Infections of the vagina and bladder are dealt with in the chapter on 'Sexually Transmitted Diseases' (page 99), although of course some of these can be acquired by women who are not sexually active. A vaginal infection is usually characterized by a sudden increase in vaginal discharge which may have a strong smell, be yellow or pink in colour rather than the normal white colour of healthy vaginal secretions, and will be accompanied by itching, soreness or redness of the vulva. Prompt medical attention should be sought. The commonest infections are the fungus called Candida (thrush) or with an organism called Trichomonas; though uncomfortable and troublesome, these are not medically serious. Gonorrhoea, on the other hand, may cause little discomfort at first but is medically serious.

Infection of the urethra (urethritis) often spreads into the bladder to cause cystitis. The symptoms are an urgent need to pass water frequently and a burning sensation while doing so. The best action to take is to drink quantities of lemon barley water and see your doctor without delay.

Sexual hygiene

Women are well advised to pass water and to wash the genitals as soon as possible after sexual intercourse to reduce the risk of infection. A bidet is ideal for this. Douching is favoured by some women but cannot be relied upon for avoiding infections – or pregnancy – and to add chemicals to the douching fluid can cause serious irritation.

Every woman should know that the risk of developing cancer of the neck of the womb (cervix) is increased by starting sexual intercourse when young and having many different sexual partners. It is believed that a virus is involved, similar to the one that causes cold sores around the mouth (herpes). The use of a sheath (condom) by the man helps to prevent the spread of sexually transmitted diseases, but remember that oral sex can also permit the passage of sexually transmitted infections.

When a woman becomes sexually aroused there is an increased flow of secretions from glands associated with the genital organs. Some women lubricate much more than others. These secretions have a distinct smell and some women use vaginal deodorants in an attempt to disguise the smell. But these deodorants can irritate and are not really necessary as the smell is perfectly natural. Sexual intercourse can be very uncomfortable if lubrication is insufficient so a lubricant jelly (such as KY) can be used or even saliva, which is always available, although this perfectly proper suggestion might perhaps offend some people's susceptibilities.

Menstrual hygiene

During their reproductive years, normal women release an egg approximately once every month. As part of this process hormones are released by the ovaries which prepare the lining of the womb to receive the egg if it is fertilized. If the egg is not fertilized the lining is shed and bleeding takes place. The blood together with bits of unwanted lining passes out through the neck of the womb and vagina – this is menstruation.

Usually this takes four or five days and then the bleeding stops as a new lining starts to build up in the womb and the whole cycle begins again. Menstrual blood does not normally clot because fibrin, which helps form the clots, is removed from the blood before it leaves the womb. In some cases, if the bleeding is rapid, this defibrination may not have time to happen and some clots may be passed – this does not necessarily mean that there is anything wrong.

Most of the myths and old wives' tales about menstruation have now disappeared and the majority of people understand that there is nothing unclean or unhealthy about this process. Indeed, there is no reason why periods should in any way affect normal everyday activities, including sporting activities.

Of course if periods are unduly heavy, painful, prolonged or are preceded by undue discomfort, medical help should be sought.

Sanitary protection

To cope with menstrual bleeding women have the choice of external or internal protection – sanitary towels or tampons – and which they use is a matter of personal choice, not only of the type, but also of the brand within each type. The manufacturers take the utmost care to see that the design and materials of their products are satisfactory and efficient and recent developments such as press-on towels have broadened the choice of product available. Ultimately, however, the choice depends upon personal preference and experience as well as the characteristics of the individual's period.

SANITARY PROTECTION

EXTERNAL

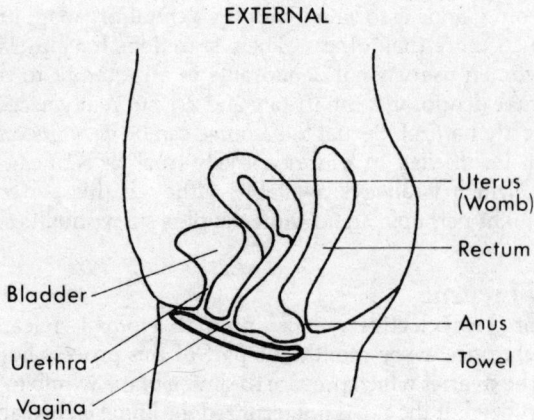

SANITARY TOWELS

OR

INTERNAL

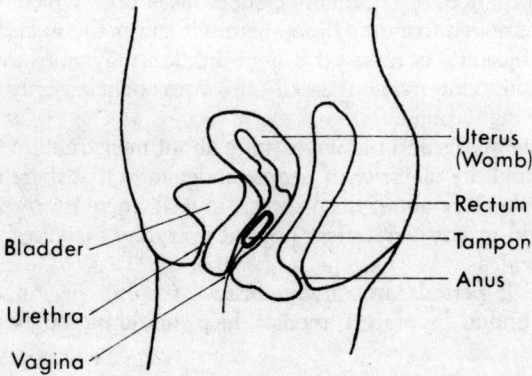

TAMPONS

External sanitary towels absorb the blood when it has passed out of the vagina. There are many types and brands available ranging from looped towels, through combined brief and towel systems, to more recent press-on towels which have adhesive strips to attach them to the inside of the panty. In addition, many of the looped and press-on brands have regular and super absorbency grades. The type used depends upon strength of flow – which varies during the period and between individuals – and personal preference. All are effective if used according to manufacturer's instructions.

It is particularly important to change towels frequently – several times per day – to avoid possible leakage, discomfort or even odour. It is helpful to wash frequently but it is not necessary to wash inside the vagina and it is certainly advisable to avoid using strong deodorants as these can cause irritation. Most modern towels are flushable but, again, the manufacturers' instructions printed on the pack indicate when the type may be flushed down the toilet. Otherwise the towel must be disposed of in an incinerator, or carefully wrapped and put in a bin.

Tampons are preferred by many women and are easily inserted into the vagina. Even most young girls are able to use tampons without any discomfort and it is important to know that the use of a tampon does not affect virginity. Again tampons are available in a range of absorbencies. Which type is used is a matter of strength of flow. Whether to use an applicator type or not is a matter of personal choice.

Tampons are felt to be more appropriate for some sporting activities, especially swimming. Exceptionally heavy flow may necessitate the use of a towel or pad in addition to a tampon during the heaviest days.

It is important to remember to remove a tampon to avoid either inserting a second one or leaving it in position for too long. In these cases an unpleasant discharge can result and occasionally an infection can follow. If this happens a doctor should be consulted immediately and recovery is usually rapid.

Regular changing is essential, three of four times a day at least, or more often during periods of heavy flow. Tampons are flushable but manufacturers' instructions should be followed regarding applicators.

Cleanliness is vital in order to avoid the transmission of germs. Hands should be washed thoroughly both before and after changing tampons.

Recently, a rare condition, called toxic shock syndrome, has attracted attention in the United States. It has been associated with tampon use and has resulted, in a few cases, in fatalities. However, the relevance of tampons is not clear because the condition has been seen in women who were not menstruating, as well as in men and children. Although there is little cause for concern because the condition is rare, should the symptoms of high fever, vomiting, diarrhoea and rash occur, the tampon should be removed and a doctor consulted immediately.

The WHC booklet, *Feminine Hygiene*, was sponsored by The Association of Sanitary Manufacturers (ASPM). It was specially written to give young girls a simple explanation of the subject. Many of them have also asked WHC for information about PMS and the menopause because they wish to help their mothers and grandmothers who may have been turned away from doctors' surgeries when they have tried to get appropriate treatment for their ills or who refuse to go and see doctors anyway. Many of these women suffer all kinds of personal and environmental problems as well. The following pages in particular should be helpful to them.

CHAPTER VII

Premenstrual syndrome and period pains

There seems to be no limit to the number of women who seek information and advice to help them with problems that can be caused by the premenstrual syndrome (PMS). However, if a woman has mental or physical problems (or both) which only occur in the second half of the menstrual cycle and cease after the period starts, then it is likely that she is suffering from a form of PMS. Some doctors still seem reluctant to recognise the existence of PMS, and of the suffering it can cause, with the result that they often complicate matters with wrong diagnoses and treatments.

The following extracts from letters written to Women's Health Concern are typical of many thousands of others we have received.

> My doctor still says it is something I have to live with but I have reached the stage where I cannot bear it any longer . . . it affects my work, social life and in fact everything. Please send me some information.

Many women believe their marriages are disrupted because of their monthly problems:

> I am 36 and have suffered PMT for years . . . my husband is in the Forces so we move about quite a lot and the doctors I see never seem to understand my problem – I leave their surgeries feeling depressed, lost and holding a prescription for tranquillizers or diuretics . . . none of the treatments I have had have helped me . . . I am fighting a losing battle and my marriage is not stable. My husband is easy-going and does not understand my problems – he feels I am awkward or sorry for myself.

Some husbands seek information to try to help their wives to get sensible advice:

> Please could you send my wife information about PMT . . . she feels helpless and believes there are no cures . . . no amount of persuasion will make her go to seek help from our doctor because she feels they don't help very much in this area.

Mothers with young children worry themselves even more about the distress they know they are inflicting on their families:

> My whole family suffers every month because of my problems . . . I went to my doctor only once because I just got tranquillizers which I could not take as they made me very sleepy and I have three children to look after.

Many women spend years trying to find the right kind of treatment for their problems. Quite often their doctors try to help them but the women themselves need to get information about PMS and the treatments being used.

> My problem is PMT. My doctor seems unable to offer any further treatment after two years of consultations. I've tried vitamin B6 and various brands of the pill. The Family Planning Clinic here can offer no other advice than to see my doctor. Please advise me what to do or who to contact with this distressing problem. I have reached a dead end with my limited knowledge.

Sometimes, when PMS sufferers have been able to learn more about the subject, they realise they need to seek further advice and possible treatment for their symptoms. Doctors are usually only too pleased to refer them elsewhere if, in fact, there is a suitable clinic or specialist within reach of their homes.

> My only regret is that I have been seeing my doctor for over two years without satisfaction for my problems and I only realised recently that the symptoms were related to my menstrual cycle . . . I am positive I'm only one in millions who is ignorant of the origin of her physical problems.
>
> It is sad I spent fifteen years being sent to different specialists on apparently dissociated ailments and nobody came up with the fact that they were all part of the same syndrome.

Millions of women have been alerted to the existence of PMS by popular publicity, but some of this has proved misleading because the attempt to simplify a complicated medical problem and simultaneously to gain popular appeal can lead to a loss of sense. Many women have labelled themselves PMT when they are not, but whatever problem they have that causes them to seek advice should be identified and properly treated.

Some medical experts are concerned that they still find it difficult to interest many of their colleagues to treat PMS. This may be because, as in many areas of illness, results are sometimes achieved and then disproved, and it is difficult to produce bio-chemical evidence. In the early 1930s medical researchers suspected that hormonal factors were causing PMS but it was not until the 1970s that they considered it to be more important to study changes in monthly hormone patterns rather than the levels. There is still no certain diagnostic test for PMS.

There is, of course, nothing new about the common monthly discomforts suffered by women. Over the whole of the female population in Britain between the ages of 14 and 50, about ten per cent have no indication that their periods are on the way and they have no cause to complain. About eighty per cent suffer more stress in the second half of the cycle but it is now possible for some of these women to avoid their recurrent difficulties. In the first place they can try a three-or-four month course of self-treatment with tablets of *pyridoxine (vitamin B6)*, as explained on page 77. These are available in chemists or health shops. Clinical trials have shown this treatment to be effective in relieving symptoms of PMS but not all women respond to it.

Another suggested self-help method which can be tried is in the form of a dietary supplement. It is gamma-linolenic acid (GLA) which is derived from the seeds of the evening primrose plant. Clinical evidence has shown that this treatment helps other conditions including eczema and some forms of alcoholism. Further medical research is being carried out to establish its possible effectiveness in relieving PMS symptoms. Some women claim to have benefitted by it when other treatments have been ineffective, and this seems to indicate that the essential fatty acids it contains are helpful to them.

Before seeking medical advice for PMS women should keep reliable monthly records of their symptoms, temperature, weight, and when their periods occur. A useful chart is shown on page 79.

Some women try to avoid their monthly problems by changing the pattern of their lives during the time in which they expect to feel irritable, tense, upset or likely to suffer a migraine headache. They stop driving their cars, take more rest, reduce their social activities and watch their diets and drinking habits. By getting to know themselves and their particular monthly patterns they can often help their situation considerably.

Our main concern at WHC is to try to help the ten per cent of women who suffer severe and sometimes long-lasting symptoms before they receive satisfactory medical advice and treatment. They need special consideration but many of them are still being neglected. They can suffer a variety of mental disturbances and physical symptoms that include breast discomfort and considerable weight gain:

I suffer from tender and 'lumpy' breasts starting around the 12–14th day of my menstrual cycle. These symptoms continue for some two weeks until they disappear at the beginning of my period.

Many women start to get PMS symptoms for the first time after having a baby:

Please help. I get dreadful anxiety and depression just before my periods, which, over the last few years and after having my babies has got much worse. I feel unbelievably tense and depressed since I had my last baby. I meditate regularly which helps with ordinary stresses and strains but doesn't help the PMT or the post-natal depression I am suffering . . . I wonder if I have an hormonal imbalance. I scream at the children and snap at my husband who has asked me to seek your help. All my problems seem to have started after the birth of our 2-year-old daughter . . . I have been to my doctor who prescribed a drug I was found to be allergic to . . . I went back to see a woman doctor who was not interested but I did not see her at my worst time. I could not struggle through a discussion and therefore 'accepted' her advice that I did not need treatment or help.

Some of the worse sufferers from PMS are over thirty-five and among those who are approaching the menopause.

I suffer terribly with migraine at period times and also at mid-cycle . . . I have tried many drugs to no avail . . . I am forty-eight now and the migraines are getting worse . . . I just go to bed for two days in agony.

I am now 42 and it is only in the last few years that I have had PMT. Prior to that all periods had been pain-free and I had none of the symptoms I get now. I had little or no sympathy for those who claimed to have any of these problems. It is amazing how experience can alter one's views drastically.

Ovulation pains

Some women ask about the pains they suffer in their mid-cycles – usually about 12–14 days after the commencement of their periods. Usually this has nothing to do with PMS but is related to ovulation. The most effective treatment is by oral contraceptives because it stops ovulation from occurring. However, if a woman is trying to have a baby she will need to discuss the matter carefully with her doctor.

PMS and crime

Stories are frequently published about women who steal goods from shops. Sometimes they have blamed PMS or some other cyclic condition.

I have been arrested for shop-lifting in the last 18 months and am rather deperate as I am suffering badly from PMT and have poor memory and concentration plus bad pain.

The WHC reply to this was to advise her not to rely on premenstrual syndrome as a defence against a charge of shoplifting, and furthermore:

The right medical specialist, we think, would be a psychiatrist to give an opinion on your memory lapses. Your GP ought to be able to refer you to a suitable psychiatrist in your area though whether this could be before your case comes up seems doubtful. Can your lawyer not ask for the case to be put back to a later date?

The credibility of PMS and women's health problems suffered a severe setback, however, in November 1981 when two women, who were on trial in criminal courts, used PMS as a legal defence for crimes they had committed. One of them was found guilty of trying to kill a policeman, having already been convicted of manslaughter after stabbing a woman to death in 1980. The second one had killed a man by running him down with a car. Both women were freed following the defendants' pleas that they acted out of character because of PMS.

A few months later PMS was used as the legal defence for the first time in the USA, and the New York District Attorney was quoted as saying that there was no scientific evidence to show that women lose the ability to know right from wrong. But PMS does have its damaging effects on some teenagers and older women – on their work, their sport, and through accidents when they are suffering the symptoms. Even so, they should be strenuously discouraged from believing they can commit crimes with impunity because of it.

Suicidal feelings

A number of women have written and telephoned WHC – sometimes in tears – saying they feel suicidal because of the PMS symptoms they are suffering and the problems they know they are making for those around them.

> I have just read an article in the Bangkok World: 'PMT – an excuse for crime?' As you say PMT doesn't make us criminals but it does change our characters for a few days and sometimes much longer . . . suicidal feelings are frequent . . . periods are prolonged . . . I haven't wanted to hurt others but I feel great despair . . . can you please send me information which might help me to help myself.

Sadly, there is little doubt that some of the unfortunate women who have committed suicide when they have been suffering from severe depression might have been helped with medical and psychiatric treatment. A mother wrote to WHC about her fears for her teenage daughter.

> My teenage daughter has tried often to take her life since she was 16 . . . she has run away and has taken pills . . . she has been in a mental hospital several times . . . I have read about someone else's daughter who had some kind of 'imbalance' which affected her and they thought

the girl was mentally ill . . . I might be clutching at straws but I just cannot sit down and wait until my daughter takes her life. She is now 17 and is in hospital again . . . I am frightened for her and for what she is doing to herself.

Suicide attempts are of course an indication of severe depression and require treatment by psychiatrists. Sometimes these severe depressive episodes are repeated in the week or ten days before each period and may then be part of the premenstrual syndrome. Treatments of various kinds may greatly help this condition, so if a girl's emotional illness recurs regularly before each period her doctor should be alerted to the possibility that she is suffering from a form of the premenstrual syndrome and needs appropriate treatment.

The WHC booklet *Premenstrual Syndrome and Period Pains* is designed to give the basic facts about PMS by answering many of the questions asked by a large number of women about it and about Period pains. These questions and answers follow:

Q. How long does PMS last in each monthly cycle?

A. *Anything from 2–14 days before the period but usually for the same number of days in any individual patient. However, the pattern may be altered if a stressful change in the patient's environment becomes apparent.*

Q. What are the main symptoms?

A. *The physical symptoms include:*
(a) *swelling of abdomen (and sometimes fingers, legs and ankles); general feeling of bloatedness;*
(b) *breast discomfort (swelling, soreness and pain);*
(c) *headaches (can be very severe and prolonged);*
(d) *backache;*
(e) *pain similar to period pain;*
(f) *skin disorders ('acne'-like blotches, etc.).*

The mental symptoms include:

(a) *tension*	*These symptoms may fluctuate in relation*
(b) *irritability*	*to each other causing a marked change in*
(c) *depression*	*personality*
(d) *lethargy*	
(e) *clumsiness*	
(f) *illogical reactions*	
(g) *lack of concentration*	
(h) *loss of confidence*	

(i)   feelings of worthlessness
(j)   loss of sex drive

Q. How many of these symptoms are usually seen and are they usually mainly physical or mental?

A. *Most patients only have a few of these symptoms, usually including depression, irritability and bloatedness with one or more other symptoms. A few unlucky patients have most of the problems in this list.*

Q. Are there other symptoms?

A. *There are some rare symptoms. If a problem starts and stops at the same time as the well-known PMS symptoms, it should be discussed with your doctor.*

Q. Are migraine, epilepsy and asthma linked in any way with PMS?

A. *These conditions often get worse in the days before the period but most doctors regard them as separate problems, which are affected by the hormonal changes near the period. In particular, migraine at this time is a separate and difficult problem for which specialised advice should be sought.*

Q. When does PMS start?

A. *Some women start PMS with their first few cycles and gradually find that it is becoming more severe. Others find that PMS starts after the birth of a baby, sometimes the first baby but not always.*

Q. How is the family affected?

A. *Unfortunately, the family often has to bear the brunt of the PMS sufferer's tension and irritability. This may show itself in arguments over sometimes trivial matters, or may explode into aggressive behaviour or even violence.*

Q. Does the husband suffer more than the children?

A. *Often yes. However, sometimes the children may be the target for verbal and physical assaults triggered off by minor misbehaviour.*

Q. Can this lead to conflict with the law?

A. *Yes, crimes of violence and theft are known to be more common among women in the premenstrual phase.*

Q. How are work, study and sport affected?

A. *Loss of all-round efficiency is common at this time. This may be due to loss of concentration and manual dexterity. Relationships with colleagues are often disrupted and PMS sufferers may refuse promotion to avoid reponsibility they fear they cannot cope with in the PMS phase. Schoolgirls and college students may find marked deterioration in their performance during the premenstrual phase. Various types of athletic performance may suffer very significantly, again due to loss of concentration and coordination.*

Q. Can the depression and associated problems of PMS lead to suicidal thoughts?

A. *Yes. This is not uncommon and urgent help may be necessary.*

Q. Does it help to have a baby?

A. *No, this is a misleading fiction. In fact existing PMS may be worse after the baby is born.*

Q. Can PMS persist after hysterectomy provided that the ovaries are left in place?

A. *Yes. The condition can become worse and is more difficult to diagnose. Specialist help may be necessary to ensure correct treatment.*

Q. Is PMS connected with period pains (dysmenorrhoea)?

A. *No. Although some women may have both PMS and severe period pains, the majority of PMS sufferers do not have marked period pains. Treatment for period pains is quite different from that for PMS (see later).*

Q. Do tranquillizers and diuretics help in PMS?

A. *Ordinary diuretics do relieve bloatedness in some cases and tranquillizers can be helpful, reducing tension in certain mild cases. However, both are now considered to be unsuitable for the management of serious cases.*

Q. What does modern treatment for PMS consist of?

A. *There are two main types:*

(a) hormonal;
(b) vitamin (pyridoxine)

Other types are used in special cases and sympathetic psychotherapy or counselling may sometimes play a useful supportive role. Brief details of the main methods are given below.

Hormonal treatment

(a) Dydrogesterone (a compound closely related to natural progesterone but with certain different properties). Taken as tablets, 10 mg twice a day from day 12 of the cycle to day 26 (Day 1 = 1st day of period) when there is a 28 day cycle. When the cycle is rather different, the doctor will adjust the timing to suit. Occasionally a slightly higher dose is needed.

(b) Norethisterone or other progesterone-like compounds may sometimes be helpful but minor side effects are more likely to be noticed.

(c) Progesterone. Suppositories containing 200 and 400mg of natural progesterone are available and are usually used for 7–14 days premenstrually.

(d) The oral contraceptive pill. The 'pill' may be effective in women who wish to use a method involving contraception and find it acceptable on medical and social grounds. In a few cases, there may be problems with depression which are difficult to deal with.

Vitamin (pyridoxine, vitamin B6) treatment

The normal dose range is 40 mg pyridoxine twice a day, rising to 75 mg twice a day in gradual steps in later cycles if necessary. The majority of PMS patients will respond to the 40 mg twice a day dose. It is very important to start the pyridoxine treatment three days before the expected start of any PMS symptoms as, if symptoms have already commenced, benefit will be much less. The tablets can be stopped 2–3 days after the start of the period. In some cases, it is useful to take an extra one or two 20 mg tablets per day just before the start of the period if the symptoms normally become more severe at that time. If you do not find improvement in the 75 mg twice a day dose, you should if possible be referred to a specialist clinic, especially if severe breast conditions or headache are main symptoms.

Common questions on PMS treatment

Q. Are there any side effects?

A. *In 5–10% of patients taking dydrogesterone there may be minor side effects, including breast tenderness, nausea and small changes in menstrual pattern.*

Minor side effects may be seen with progesterone suppositories. The side effects of the contraceptive pill are outside the scope of this booklet but full advice can be obtained from your own doctor or a Family Planning Association (FPA) Clinic.

There are no established side effects with pyridoxine unless the recommended dose level is exceeded, i.e. when 100 mg twice a day is taken there may be some gastric 'acidity' or nausea.

Q. Are these treatments 100% effective?

A. *No treatment is 100% effective but, if used properly, dydrogesterone and pyridoxine should both bring relief to at least 75% of patients. Response rates for other treatments are difficult to assess but progesterone suppositories and the 'pill' undoubtedly have a very useful success rate.*

Q. What happens if I am one of the 25% who do not respond to dydro-gesterone or pyridoxine?

A. *The first step is usually for the doctor to try pyridoxine if dydrogester-one was used first, or vice versa. If relief is still not adequate, a combination of pyridoxine and dydrogesterone may be more helpful than either singly.*
  Your doctor may wish to refer you to a specialist clinic at this point and certainly this is desirable if the combination gives unsatisfactory results.
  The specialist PMS clinic will then carry out a detailed reinvestigation, including special hormone tests. They may then consider the use of special drugs such as bromocryptin and danazol, some of which are normally only available to hospital doctors. Research continues and new treatments are under investigation.

Q. What can I do to help my doctor in treating my PMS?

A. *It is very helpful if the patient keeps accurate records of her symptoms in relation to her monthly cycle. Details of her period (duration, character of the flow, etc.) and any symptoms experienced around the time of ovulation are also helpful. These records may help to convince any doctor who may be in doubt about the regular cyclical nature of your symptoms.*

Q. What do I do if my doctor wishes to continue to use tranquillizers and diuretics only?

A. *This can be a difficult situation. A tactful approach from you requesting a referral to a PMS clinic or a gynaecologist may help.*

Q. How can I find the address of a PMS Clinic in my area?

A. *There are still very few specialist PMS Clinics although a number of gynaecologists will give expert advice. You should try to talk to your own doctor first and ask about details of possible facilities in your area.*

MENSTRUAL CHART PMS

Indicate on the chart the days on which symptoms trouble you using the appropriate letter or letters from the key below.
Also mark the days of the menstrual flow (M). Please punctuate carefully to avoid any confusion.

Fill in months (e.g. May)

Days of the month

| 1 | 2 | 3 | 4 | 5 | 6 | 7 | 8 | 9 | 10 | 11 | 12 | 13 | 14 | 15 | 16 | 17 | 18 | 19 | 20 | 21 | 22 | 23 | 24 | 25 | 26 | 27 | 28 | 29 | 30 | 31 |

1st Month

(...............)

2nd Month

(...............)

3rd Month

(...............)

Key to symptoms

Depression - D	Swollen ankles or fingers - F	Loss of sex drive - LS
Irritability (tension) - I	Headache - H	Period pains - PP
Lethargy (tiredness) - T	Increased appetite - AP	Nausea - N
Breast discomfort - B	Lack co-ordination (clumsiness) - C	Menstrual flow - M
Swollen abdomen - A	Back ache - BA	

79

Period pains

Many women experience some pain and other discomforts on the day before the period starts and on the first day of the menstrual flow. These 'period pains', or *dysmenorrhoea* as the condition is known medically, often warrant the use of *aspirin* or similar proprietary analgesics (pain killers). However, in some cases the pain may be severe and accompanied by nausea and vomiting. Women and girls so affected may feel obliged to take to their beds, with consequent loss of time at work or school. Schoolgirls and young women are the most common sufferers.

It is important to realise that period pains and premenstrual tension are two quite separate conditions.

Here are some of the most common questions asked about period pains and WHC's answers.

Q. What type of pain is most common?

A. *Typically, the pain is spasmodic, starting in the flanks, coming to the middle of the lower abdomen, and may then be referred to the upper inner parts of the thighs.*

Q. When is the condition most common?

A. *Though the first few periods experienced by a young girl may be painless, period pains may soon show themselves and the condition is considered to be most common in late teens and early 20's.*

It should gradually begin to become unimportant by the late 20's, or earlier if there is a pregnancy, especially one leading to the vaginal delivery of a normal size baby.

Q. Is any particular type of girl especially prone to period pains?

A. *It is generally believed that those who are rather introspective and less physically active are more liable, but this is not easy to prove.*

Q. Is there any psychological basis for period pain?

A. *The most common form of period pain (spasmodic dysmenorrhoea) is associated with the release of a chemical called prostaglandin by the womb which leads to contraction of the womb muscle. The sensitivity of the individual to the pain caused by these conditions may sometimes be affected by the woman's psychological state.*

Another kind of severe period pain (secondary dysmenorrhoea) is associated with various gynaecological conditions, such as endometriosis and pelvic inflammatory disease. There is obviously a clear physical cause for the pain.

However, some authorities hold that there are a few women who experience period pains for which neither of these explanations is acceptable and therefore they consider that there may be a real psychological basis for their pains.

Q. Can the doctor find any abnormalities on clinical examinations?

A. *No abnormality is seen in young women with period pains, but sometimes pain at the time of the period in older women can be associated with abnormal physical findings, such as endometriosis, pelvic inflammatory disease and fibroids.*

Q. What should be done if aspirin or some other analgesic, or rest and warmth do not help?

A. *Your doctor may wish to use antispasmodic drugs and if the pain is very severe and disabling, the new anti-prostaglandin drugs such as mefanamic acid, flufenamic acid and flurbiprofen may be employed.*

The doctor will wish to exclude any physical abnormalities before using these drugs.

If you are prepared to accept the oral contraceptive pill, good results, are usually obtained, due to the major changes in the hormonal environment which are imposed.

Courses of a hormone preparation, the synthetic progestogen compound dydrogesterone sometimes give useful results.

Q. What is the position of the older woman (aged 25–50 years) who has more prolonged pain and other discomforts, either before the period or during it?

A. *As previously mentioned, there can be a number of causes for pain and this type of discomfort, some of which are mentioned above.*

You should see your own doctor in the first instance. The doctor may treat you or refer you to a gynaecologist. Many of these conditions can be effectively dealt with, especially if they are not neglected by the patient.

CHAPTER VIII

The menopause and later years

The word 'menopause' refers to the cessation of menstruation. The correct medical term for the change of life is the 'climacteric'. By common usage, however, menopause has come to encompass all the changes which a woman undergoes at that time.

The letters and telephone inquiries which reach Women's Health Concern regularly give a clear indication of the personal problems that affect many women undergoing the menopause – and the attitudes that are still being adopted by some of the doctors they consult:

> I find it difficult to discuss menopause with my doctor . . . doctors can be kind and sympathetic as people but one request for medical help was answered: 'Yes my wife suffers from it but she is very good and never complains'.

> I have been to see my doctor determined to get a referral letter six times and each time I have come out without one . . . it is difficult to change after a lifetime of believing your doctor must be right and to start to tell him you think you know better than he does what is wrong with you.

> I am writing about my mother who is 47 and has been suffering all the normal symptoms of the menopause . . . she also suffers insomnia and feels that her family and friends are against her . . . During the past two years she has deteriorated so much and has withdrawn from seeing people . . . if we mention a doctor or tablets she goes into crying fits and refuses to go to get any medical advice . . . I have been to see the doctor about it and he says he cannot help us unless she consults him . . . can you please tell me what to do?

> I desperately need to talk to someone who is sympathetic and at the same time constructive as communication for me is difficult on personal issues. Can you put me in touch with a qualified counsellor?

> Many thanks for your constructive information about oestrogen/ progestogen treatments. I am now taking this type of treatment and can cope so much better with my job, family and other commitments.

The woman today who is approaching the menopause, or has already passed it, is more fortunate than were her female ancestors who – until fifty or sixty years ago – often died before their reproductive years were over.

Now that the average lifespan of women has increased to well past seventy years – which means that many will live for twenty to thirty years or longer after their menopause – the proper use and acceptance of modern treatment for women who need it can help them to enjoy good physical and mental health in their later years, and this can include the continuation of a satisfactory sex life. In fact, after the menopause, many women find a new level of contentment in their lives.

By providing up-to-date information to women and doctors on the proper use of oestrogen-progestogen and other treatments and relevant facts concerning women's conditions WHC has helped to put some of the controversies into perspective. For instance, the biggest setback to the advance of the proper use of oestrogen therapy (see below page 88) was the much publicised evidence relating unopposed oestrogen treatment to an increased risk of womb cancer in the USA in 1975. Medical workers provided evidence that the addition of progestogen to part of the oestrogen course avoided this risk. International medical opinion now considers this combined treatment to be safe and it is the most effective therapy for treating menopause symptoms and for helping post-menopausal women to prevent certain forms of heart disease, cancer of the womb, circulatory problems, bone deterioration (osteoporosis) and other undesirable changes.

Oestrogen treatment should be prescribed only when the doctor is reasonably certain that a woman's symptoms are due to oestrogen deficiency. In general, low doses are prescribed at first to try to control common symptoms – hot flushes, vaginal discomfort, lack of concentration and other problems. If necessary, doctors can increase the dosage until the woman feels better. Many doctors then decide to stop treatment gradually, perhaps over 18–24 months. But for the many women who may suffer painful fractures easily and frequently in later years, there is every good reason why treatment should be continued, under medical supervision – perhaps for the rest of their lives if they so wish (see page 86).

Professor Gilbert Gordan carried out a study from 1948 to 1973 on 220 post-menopausal women using oestrogen therapy. He said: 'This is an enormous health problem, the No. 12 cause of death in the United States . . . women start to lose bone mass at age 50 and drop 50 per cent bone mass by 70 as opposed to men who lose only 25 per cent by 90 . . . fractures are preventable with small amounts of oestrogens'.

Mr Malcolm Whitehead, the gynaecologist who directs the menopause clinics at King's College Hospital and the Chelsea Hospital for Women in London, has also said: 'In many developed countries the total cost of treating osteoporosis and related fractures is very high. For example, there are 6.4 million post-menopausal women aged over sixty years in Britain and the financial consequences of fractures of the neck of the femur (hip) alone are in this group, at least £100 million a year – in the USA the figure exceeds $1 billion a year'.

This is, in fact, the fifth most expensive item for Britain's national health service. Malcolm Whitehead believes that a future development will enable all women to be screened after the menopause to find out who would be likely to suffer substantial osteoporosis. It seems that women often break their wrists over the age of fifty-five and, as they grow older, the risk of breaking their shoulders and hips increases. At least 25 per cent of those over sixty suffer vertebral compression due to deterioration of bones in the spine which causes severe back problems and broken bones. Apparently black women suffer less osteoporosis than white women and this seems to be the case whether they live in Africa or in other countries.

The major problem for doctors who prescribe hormone treatments is to determine whether psychological disturbances are due to oestrogen deficiency or to different kinds of breakdown in women's lives. Many women are confused by popular publicity that can mislead them and their families into blaming their problems on the menopause or some other hormone imbalance. Sometimes their problems are due to other disease conditions, environmental and personal stresses, or ageing processes. Many of them still lack the basic knowledge they need to care for themselves and they persist in, for example, bad diet, excessive smoking, drinking or drug-taking. Sometimes counselling and psychotherapy are more important than hormonal treatment and there are of course some women who, for medical reasons, must not use oestrogens because in their cases unacceptable risks (described on page 89) would be entailed.

It is, however, increasingly evident that large numbers of women who suffer from menopause symptoms and those who want to try to preserve their good health in later years are still being neglected. Doctors who refuse to prescribe the much-tested oestrogen/progestogen treatments sometimes issue all kinds of other prescriptions that are considered by experts to be ineffective and even dangerous. For instance, certain types of contraceptive pills containing high levels of *synthetic* oestrogens, which are necessary to prevent ovulation, are irrelevant and are considered to be hazardous for women over the age of thirty-five. Tranquillizers over a long period can also be the cause of unpleasant side-effects and can lead to addiction.

Many women try to inform themselves by reading books about the menopause and through information gleaned from newspapers, magazines, radio and television. Many are still turned away from out-dated practices where they may even have been told – sometimes by receptionists – that they might get cancer if they go to menopause clinics! Such mis-information is upsetting for women, who may eventually give up the struggle to get the right kind of medical advice, while others look for doctors who will be able to consider their symptoms seriously and treat them appropriately, or send them to clinics or consultants* for proper assessment.

*See lists of clinics, page 149.

The WHC booklet *The Menopause* explains the function of the two sex hormones, oestrogen and progesterone, and why oestrogen levels decrease at the time of the menopause and afterwards. It defines the true menopause symptoms. It refers to osteoporosis and to hysterectomy and depression. It explains the proper use of oestrogen therapy (commonly called hormone replacement therapy – HRT) and the importance of good counselling.

The menopause usually occurs between the ages of forty and fifty-five and can take place at any earlier age and sometimes later. The menopausal problems that a woman may have can occur at the time of the climacteric or afterwards in the post-menopausal years. To appreciate the reason for this, it is necessary to understand what happens to the woman's sex hormones.

Hormones

Hormones are naturally occurring chemical substances produced by various glands in the body. They circulate in the blood stream and act on other parts of the body. There are many different hormones with a great variety of actions.

OESTROGEN and PROGESTERONE are the female sex hormones and are produced in a woman's body by the ovaries. The cells which manufacture them develop in association with the ripening egg cells. All the egg cells a woman will ever have are present in an immature form before she is born. No new egg cells are produced after birth and when the supply of these eggs runs out the menopause occurs. Before the menstrual periods (monthly bleeds) finally cease the amount of oestrogen being produced starts to fall and this may cause menopausal symptoms while the woman is still menstruating.

It is the action of oestrogen which causes the changes that occur when a girl develops into a woman at puberty. Her breasts enlarge, her body contours become rounded and the reproductive organs increase in size. Oestrogen and progesterone acting together are responsible for the monthly growth of the lining of the womb. A sharp fall in the circulating levels of these two hormones causes the lining to be shed as the menstrual period. Throughout their reproductive years healthy women have more-or-less regular monthly bleeds. A lack of oestrogen can cause the vagina to become dry, less supple and more prone to infection. This may lead to painful sexual intercourse. It also results in a shrinkage of the womb and breasts. Prolapse of the womb and vagina and sagging of the breasts are aggravated by the loss of elasticity of the supporting tissues caused by oestrogen lack. Hot flushes and sweating are characteristic symptoms of a lowered level of oestrogen. It is, however, important to understand that this decrease in oestrogen level at the menopause is normal and occurs in every woman. It is only those women complaining of specific ill-effects who can be said to be suffering from the menopausal syndrome. Other women who at this time do not experience troublesome symptoms find it difficult to understand, or even believe, the complaints of genuine sufferers.

Men do not normally have a change of life in their middle years that can be compared with a woman's menopause as the testes (the male equivalent of the ovaries) continue to manufacture sperms and male hormones into old age in most cases but general ageing processes are inevitable in both sexes.

The menopausal syndrome

The effects that the menopause has on women vary widely. In fact, for each woman it is an individual experience. Many have little or no trouble at all. Some never even have hot flushes. In others, the flushes may last for a few days or many years. The average time is a few months.

The true menopausal symptoms include: hot flushes, night sweats causing insomnia and tiredness, joint pains, dryness of the vagina and painful sexual intercourse. Irritability, mild depression and impairment of memory and concentration are also common.

Hot flushes affect women in different ways. They usually are experienced in the upper part of the body, neck and head. They may or may not be visible to other people. They vary in frequency from only an occasional one to many times during the day and night. At night, they usually result in excessive sweating which can disrupt sleep for the sufferer and – if she shares a double bed – for her partner as well. Women at work feel embarrassed when they occur in the presence of other people. These unpleasant symptoms can cause tiredness, inefficiency at work and disharmony at home.

The flushes and the associated nervous symptoms usually disappear after a variable time but the vaginal changes do not resolve and similar changes may affect the bladder, causing frequency and urgency of the desire to pass water. The skin and hair may become dryer and the nails tend to break.

Osteoporosis – bone deterioration

Osteoporosis or thinning of the bones is a process which occurs to a variable extent in all women following the menopause. This results in a progressive increase in the rate of fractures of the wrist and hip. It also causes loss of height and bending of the spine as a result of compression of the bones of the vertebral column. Fractures of the hip are a major cause of death in elderly ladies. It is now quite clear that osteoporosis can be prevented by prolonged oestrogen therapy.

Depression

Many women, at the time of the menopause, feel depressed and less well than before.

In some the depression is a direct result of the menopausal syndrome. These women may feel they cannot manage their jobs or cope with their everyday affairs, because of poor memory and lack of concentration. This damages their self-confidence. The usual mild form of depression thus caused will disappear as the menopausal symptoms are relieved.

However, if a woman has suffered from previous bouts of depression, such as post-natal depression, a more severe form of depression may occur around the time of the menopause and this usually requires psychiatric as well as hormonal treatment.

Others may feel bored or unwanted because their children have grown up and they seem to be deprived of a worthwhile role in life. They feel isolated with nobody to talk to. For many, the menopause occurs at the time of life when there are special social and domestic problems. There may be marital or other relationship stresses or associated troubles with children. There may be grief over the loss of a parent or the demands of looking after sick, elderly relations. There may be financial or legal problems. What they need could be a new approach to life. They should be encouraged to take up new activities, particularly those which will enable them to meet people. A part-time or even full-time job is often the answer though this should not be so strenuous or time-consuming that it interferes with good relationships with husbands, children and friends. A proper balance between work and relaxation is important. It is often a time to develop new leisure interests. These are the people who can be helped by discussion of their problems with a counsellor.

How to get help

In the first place you could help yourself by coming to terms with inevitable changes that have taken place in your body and possibly in your life. There are advantages, such as freedom from fear of unwanted pregnancies. A positive approach to the years ahead can be very beneficial. You should not hesitate to consult your doctor about your problem. Many women who are approaching or have reached the age of the menopause feel inclined to blame this for a whole variety of symptoms which in fact have nothing to do with it. Unfortunately some doctors are inclined to do this too. It must be stressed that the menopausal syndrome is a relatively specific condition for which there is specific treatment. Many women who attend menopause clinics turn out to have premenstrual syndrome, psychiatric illness, or marital problems as well as various other causes for their symptoms. A skilled doctor should be able to discover whether the problem is related to the menopause or not. When there is doubt whether there are menopausal hormone changes a blood test may be performed to measure follicle stimulating hormone (FSH). The level of this hormone rises when the ovaries begin to fail and stays high following the menopause. If the symptoms can be attributed to oestrogen lack the doctor may prescribe hormone therapy. Otherwise counselling or other medical help may be recommended.

General counselling and psychotherapy

Women's Health Concern encourages doctors and nurses to become good counsellors. Trained nurse-counsellors can advise women about their general health and the cyclic disturbances that may cause suffering at the time of the menopause. Provided the counsellors have the support of the doctors, they can ensure that women get adequate medical supervision and ease the workload in busy GP's practices and in surgeries in large industrial companies.

For those who need psychotherapy and the deeper analysis it usually involves, it is important they should attend therapists who are able to assess them properly and continue with regular sessions long enough for useful results to be achieved.

Oestrogen therapy

This treatment (commonly called HRT – hormone replacement therapy) is appropriate if there are symptoms of oestrogen lack and can lead to dramatic improvement. There is now no need for a woman to have to accept a significant deterioration in the quality of her life or to have to put up with painful intercourse or even stop it altogether because of oestrogen lack. However, though oestrogen alleviates the symptoms, in recent years doctors have shown that, if given alone in some women it may over-stimulate the lining of the womb. This can cause abnormal bleeding and increase the risk of cancer of the lining of the womb. It is therefore now recommended that oestrogen treatment – particularly for women who have not undergone hysterectomy – should normally be accompanied by a progestogen (a progesterone-like drug) taken for at least ten days a month. At the end of each cycle of treatment the lining of the womb breaks down after a few days and is shed as a withdrawal bleed – usually rather scanty. Women having this type of combined therapy seem to have a lower risk of womb cancer than women on no treatment at all. Though with this treatment you can expect to have regular withdrawal bleeds, this does not mean you are again liable to become pregnant. Some women do not have withdrawal bleeds even with the combined treatment; this does not matter as it means that the oestrogen dosage being taken is causing insufficient growth of the lining of the womb for the progestogen withdrawal to result in bleeding and this is quite safe.

Hormone preparations

The brand names given in this section are those available in Britain. The combined preparations are not available in all countries but doctors can prescribe the separate ingredients.

There are a variety of hormone preparations available. In general, doctors prescribe the lowest effective dose of whichever treatment they choose. If the response is unsatisfactory, the dose may be changed or another preparation can be tried.

The oestrogens are classified as synthetic (made in the laboratory) such as ethinyl oestradiol; and naturally occurring such as are in Premarin, Harmogen and Progynova. Some doctors believe that the naturally occurring oestrogens (which are more expensive) are safer because they are not likely to cause blood clotting (thrombosis); others think there is no difference and that, at the low dosage used for treating menopause symptoms, the risk is minimal anyway.

Combined preparations such as Prempak, Cycloprogynova, Menophase and Trisequens include a progestogen and are put up in packages that provide different formulations and treatment patterns in monthly cycles. With all such treatments withdrawal bleeding usually occurs shortly after the progestogen tablets have been taken. Though some doctors prefer to prescribe treatment that gives the woman a one-week break in hormone treatment during which time she has her bleed, others prefer continuous treatment without a break. The doctor's skill consists in prescribing treatment that is effective, appropriate for the individual woman and safe.

More reasons for treatment

There is a particularly strong case for oestrogen therapy in women who have had an early menopause, whether naturally occurring or following the surgical removal of the ovaries. A history of osteoporosis in the family is another good reason for this type of treatment.

When oestrogen treatment is not advised

There are a number of medical conditions which may make oestrogen treatment too risky for safety so that in the presence of these, most doctors would be unwilling to prescribe it. They include cancer of the reproductive organs and breasts (even if treated by surgery with or without radiotherapy), previous deep vein thrombosis, certain forms of liver disease in which oestrogen can cause jaundice, marked obesity and certain types of high blood pressure. Though oestrogen tablets by mouth may not be allowed in these conditions, oestrogen cream can still be used for vaginal symptoms if necessary, but it should be realised that some absorption of oestrogen can take place so that the use of the cream should be sparing and strictly in accordance with doctors instructions. Other treatments can have some effect on the remaining menopausal symptoms. They are, however, less reliable in relieving symptoms than oestrogens so that a small number of patients with contra-indications to oestrogen treatment unfortunately fail to get satisfactory relief. Homoeopathic medicine, dietary supplements, acupuncture and so forth all have their advocates but there is no scientific evidence that they really help.

Hysterectomy and oöphorectomy
(removal of ovaries)

Total hysterectomy is removal of the entire uterus (womb) and will stop menstruation immediately. If the ovaries are conserved, menopausal symptoms will not occur. If, however, the ovaries are removed before the menopause there will be a sudden cessation of oestrogen production and this is usually associated with acute menopausal symptoms.

These operations should, of course, not be done without good reason, such as the removal of diseased structures, the treatment of persistent heavy periods or as part of the treatment for cancer. For many women, following removal of the ovaries but not necessarily after hysterectomy, oestrogen therapy will be appropriate and some gynaecologists insert a pellet of hormones (an implant) under the skin at the time of the operation.

Women are strongly advised to talk to their gynaecologists and to ask them all the questions they need to be answered both before and after operation. Women's Health Concern receives a large number of inquiries from women who want to know how long it may take them to make a total recovery, about their sex lives, how long the effects of an implant may last, what should happen afterwards and so on. All the answers and any other information should be available from the gynaecologists treating them and women could save themselves a lot of unnecessary worry if they would follow such advice.

Sterilisation

A sterilisation operation only blocks the fallopian tubes and has no effect on hormone production. There are no after-effects of sterilisation except in a few women whose periods become heavier. Some of these were previously using oral contraceptives (the pill) which tend to produce light menstrual periods anyway.

Heart attacks and the menopause

Younger women are less likely than men of comparable age to suffer from coronary heart disease (heart attacks) but from the age of about 45 onwards the chance of a woman having a heart attack gradually increases to approach that of a man of similar age. If a woman loses her ovaries when young (or they fail to develop and function normally) the risk of heart disease at a given age is more like that of men than of women. It is generally believed that female hormones are protective and their deficiency leads to loss of that protection. High levels of blood fats (lipids and cholesterol) also increase the risk of heart attacks. These levels tend to rise after the menopause but again, female hormones tend to protect against a rise in lipid levels.

Questions and answers on the menopause

Can oestrogen therapy be dangerous? No medical treatment is completely free of side-effects or complications. If you have had breast or womb cancer, a thrombosis, have high blood pressure or are seriously overweight, your doctor may decide it is inadvisable to give you hormones.

The dose of oestrogen given is considerably less than that in the contraceptive pill, which means that the risk of thrombosis is less; some doctors consider there is no thrombosis risk. It is now well established that oestrogen therapy, which is one of the most carefully investigated forms of medical treatment, is safe when properly prescribed and supervised.

How long should I take oestrogen therapy? You probably need to take it for at least several months and many women take it for years under medical supervision. It is best to reduce the dosage gradually rather than to stop suddenly. The latter tends to result in a return of the symptoms. Your doctor will advise you on this. In practice, doctors vary the type of treatment and the length of time it is continued according to the individual's response. There are arguments for keeping the treatment going for the rest of a woman's life, but some doctors argue against this. If it is being used to prevent osteoporosis it will need to be taken indefinitely.

Will oestrogen therapy improve my desire for sex? It will cure the pain at intercourse caused by a dry vagina and this, with an improvement in your general well-being, improves the sexual desire in many cases. There may, however, still be problems for which expert medical advice should be sought. Individuals vary but a gradual decline in the need for sex is normal in many men and women and should be accepted gracefully.

Is a woman ever too old to benefit from oestrogen therapy? No, age is no reason for not having this type of treatment, even many years after the menopause, if symptoms of oestrogen lack are present.

Are menstrual disturbances symptomatic of the menopause? Only a decrease in frequency and cessation of periods can be due to the menopause. Heavy, prolonged or frequent periods should be discussed with your doctor who will usually seek the opinion of a gynaecologist. The same applies if bleeding occurs more than six months after the periods have apparently stopped, or if there is irregular bleeding while taking treatment.

When can I stop using contraceptive measures? Fertility decreases steadily after the age of forty, but a woman who is having spontaneous periods is potentially fertile. The usual advice is that contraception should be used until two years after the periods cease. However, it is unlikely that a woman with menopausal symptoms, such as hot flushes, and whose periods have ceased for several months, will be able to conceive.

Special tests measuring follicle stimulating hormone (FSH) in the blood can, if high, indicate that pregnancy is no longer likely to be possible.

What are fibroids and how does the menopause affect them? Fibroids are non-cancerous lumps caused by swelling of the muscle and fibrous tissue of the womb. In some women they give rise to no symptoms and do not need treatment; in others the lumps will either be removed on their own (myomectomy) or a hysterectomy may be necessary.

After the menopause fibroids usually get smaller and may shrink up completely. However, with oestrogen treatment there is some risk that they may not shrink or may even enlarge.

I have read about the possible use of a new type of cream or sticky plasters for treating the menopause. Can you please enlighten me? French research workers have developed a cream containing oestrogen in a hydro-gel base called (oestrogel) which, when rubbed into the skin, allows the oestrogel to pass directly into the blood stream without having first to go through the liver, as happens when tablets are taken. This may have advantages for women with certain medical conditions (such as a history of previous blood clots) and research is being carried out at King's College Hospital in London to check on this. At present (1984), the cream is not licensed by the Medicines Commission and so it is not available on prescription in the UK. In general, the effects of the cream are believed to be similar to tablets and implants, and, like these, will not suit all women. It is not directly beneficial to the skin itself. It would seem that the cream has to be applied daily to an area of skin on the body (not the face) about one foot square (900cm.sq.) which some women find undoubtedly tedious and it gives off a smell of alcohol when being rubbed in.

Plasters that will adhere to the skin and provide this type of gel in a special container with a permeable membrane may deliver a more exactly measured dose and may become available for future use. For the majority of women, however, menopause symptoms are most conveniently treated by tablets because control of the dosage is easier than with other methods.

CHAPTER IX

Post-natal depression

There is nothing new about the 'maternal blues' or, to give it its official description, post-natal depression – those symptoms we know as feelings of anxiety, of inadequacy, and of isolation, coupled with exhaustion and tearfulness. What *is* new is that we now recognise this condition, and that in modern society families are often so split up that a new mother may no longer have the reliable and present support of mother, sisters, and aunts and often has to cope with her difficulties on her own. When she needs it most, loving care may be hard to find. Her husband may be out working, or in the case of one-parent families is sometimes 'not there' – and either way there may be financial worries to add to lack of emotional support. Add the bodily hormonal changes that occur during childbirth, with perhaps a few personal hang-ups to add to the fears, the isolation and the exhaustion and these are the conditions to produce post-natal depression.

With good hospital care and the loving support of husband and friends, these symptoms may not develop into anything serious. But for an unlucky few without such support – and with perhaps a predisposition to depression anyway – it may turn into a full-scale depression lasting from weeks to months and needing expert care. In these cases both mother and baby may be at risk, so expert medical help is needed *urgently*.

Most mild cases may need only anti-depressant tablets to tide them over this bad patch, while more severe cases may need hospital treatment. Some modern hospitals take in both mother and baby so that neither suffers from maternal deprivation. Treatment in hospital may take the form of drugs (anti-depressants), other medical treatment and psychotherapy, or 'talking treatment', in which the patient talks to a sympathetic therapist, either in a group or individually, and together they try to find out what is at the root of the trouble. This is not a frightening ordeal – on the contrary it can be a rewarding and enriching experience – and it is essential for the sake of the baby to obtain help as soon as possible, for an unresponsive, depressed mother is bound to have an effect on a baby's developing personality. Usually it is helpful to involve the Health Visitor or another nurse who knows the woman's background and circumstances. More often than not it is necessary to see a doctor who will try to treat the woman with appropriate medication or refer her for psychiatric treatment.

Woman's Health Concern receives many letters and calls from unhappy women who believe they are still suffering from post-natal depression and from many near to them who want to help them with their babies. One worried husband, for example, wrote as follows:

> I am writing to ask your advice about post-natal illness suffered by my wife who has been treated for this condition after the birth of our two children. Although the doctor has helped tremendously and is understanding, she is still not better. My questions never seem to get answered . . . How long does it last? . . . Can you help us? . . . we have no real problems and everything around the family is very good.

WHC replied:

> Depression – except when due to obvious causes such as grief from loss of a near relative or a personal calamity – is often difficult to understand. This is true of post-natal depression which, although triggered by the dramatic body changes associated with childbirth, occurs in some women only, despite the fact that childbirth causes similar body changes in all women. The brain chemistry in those affected is disturbed in such a way as to lead to depression . . . Recovery is the rule but the time taken for recovery is variable and difficult to predict. Usually anti-depressant drugs help to speed it up. Sometimes the shake-up produced by ECT (electro-convulsive therapy known as 'shock treatment') restores normal brain function. The psychotherapy that an understanding and sympathetic counsellor can give often helps a great deal. As your wife seems to be in the care of such a doctor, the best you can do is to accept his advice and leave him to do as much as he can to help her.

There are many different thoughts in women's minds when they are trying to find answers for the set-backs they seem to be suffering after the birth of their babies. One mother wrote to us:

> My child is eleven months only and I have suffered depressions which are becoming more increasingly severe. They seem to be linked, in part at least with my menstrual cycle which was only re-established three months ago. Before my pregnancy I was on the Pill and had been for 12 years and I wonder whether my body is recovering from these years as well as the pregnancy.

The WHC reply said:

> Use of the pill before pregnancy has nothing to do with subsequent post-natal depression for which, of course, you should contact your doctor and if it is sufficiently severe, be referred for specific evaluation. Your letter suggests that you might be experiencing a form of premenstrual syndrome.

During pregnancy, most women feel happy and well after they have got over the early stage when so many feel sick. Consultations with doctors and admissions to hospital for emotional illness are proportionately fewer than for non-pregnant women. But after delivery there is a sharp rise in these consultations and admissions. There are grounds for believing that some of the freedom from nervous illnesses during pregnancy and their increased frequency afterwards are related to the profound and very complicated hormone changes which occur.

Dr Gerald Swyer explains it in the WHC booklet on post-natal depression:

In the course of pregnancy there is a great increase in the production of the female hormones, *oestrogen* and *progesterone*, which bring about the growth of the uterus to accommodate the growing fetus and, together with a hormone from the pituitary gland, *prolactin*, which also circulates in increased amounts, prepare the breasts for subsequent milk secretion.

An entirely new hormone, *chorionic gonadotrophin*, produced by the embryonic tissue, circulates in the mother's blood from the time the fertilized egg is implanted in the lining of the uterus. Once the placenta (afterbirth) is established it too secretes hormones into the maternal blood, some of which, like chorionic gonadotrophin, are peculiar to pregnancy. Studies of animal behaviour lead us to believe that some, if not all of the hormones have effects on the brain, leading to modifications of behaviour. Some of these, like nesting behaviour, are obvious and well known. Others still require much study for their full elucidation.

In humans, the organisation of the brain and its functions are far more complex than in other animals and behaviour is believed to be mainly the result of pure mental or brain activity, affected far more by the physical environment in which the person lives and by thought processes, than by circulating chemical substances in the blood such as hormones. Nevertheless, the influence of these chemicals in certain circumstances is undeniable and therefore it would be a mistake to underestimate their importance in modifying human behaviour.

At the end of the pregnancy, with delivery of the baby, another set of profound hormone changes occur, with precipitate falls of female hormone levels and the disappearance, after a few days, of chorionic gonadotrophin and the other placental special hormones. Prolactin, on the other hand, remains high to permit milk secretion. Knowing what we do, from animal studies for example, about the changes in behaviour brought about by hormones, it would be surprising if the dramatic alteration in hormone status following delivery did not have some effect on a woman's emotional state. However, though all pregnant women experience these hormone changes, only a minority have emotional problems after childbirth, so clearly other factors must be involved.

These certainly include the woman's emotional make-up and the various experiences she encountered before becoming pregnant, but it must freely be admitted that we do not understand precisely why some women are and others are not affected in this way.

Some women torment themselves with different self-imposed worries which they develop before and after they have had their babies. In some cases they can be helped by talking to a good psychotherapist. Mrs Irene Swyer is one of the practitioners in London who has tried to use her professional skills in this way. In the same WHC booklet, she explains how and why many of them worry about their babies:

Many women worry whether all is well with the baby. Is he 'all right'?; is he perhaps a mongol? If the risk, in her case, of having an abnormal baby is sufficiently great, her obstetrician would no doubt advise her on the desirability of undergoing tests to see if the embryo is normal or not. Unless one has actually experienced giving birth to a baby, the confinement can be fraught with fantasies and anxieties due to tales that have been told, particularly if the woman's mother has elaborated about her own sufferings. This in itself can be a predisposing cause for anxiety and depression when the mother-to-be has grown up hearing what pain she is supposed to have caused her own mother.

She may have preconceived ideas about whether she will definitely breast feed or bottle feed. Inability to breast feed in these cases often produces an intense feeling of failure, frequently reinforced by the husband and others. Assurance is needed that bottle-fed babies do just as well as long as they have lots of cuddling. Good ante-natal care, which all women are entitled to, should include not only physical supervision, relevant advice about vitamins, the harmfulness of smoking and so on, but also the reassurance that most expectant mothers so badly need.

The possible causes for women's depressions after the birth of their babies are, of course, many. Irene Swyer believes many different factors to be relevant:

The basic relations of the couple is of prime importance, their maturity and whether their sexual relationship is good or otherwise; do they both want the baby?; did one and not the other?; or did it just 'happen'?; are there strong feelings about what sex the baby should be?; and how mixed are the feelings of the mother about this new person growing within her? She may on the one hand be very pleased, but these feelings of pleasure may well be over-ridden by other feelings which make her experience guilt and resentment. This new member of the family who is taking over, perhaps by making her feel sick and wretched, is changing her figure, causing her clothes no longer to fit; who is very likely creating a need for enlarged living accommodation, along with a greatly increased financial expenditure which may coincide with a reduction in the couple's income due to the wife's having to give up work. This, she may well be reluctant to do as besides losing her financial independence, she may bitterly resent having to forego the company of the people with whom she has been working. More seriously, she may be worried about losing her step on the promotional ladder.

Many women would still prefer to give birth to their babies in their own homes but this is not always practical and it is generally accepted that most of them receive better medical treatment by going to hospital. Unfortunately it too often happens that the hospital staff, no matter how well-meaning, create a situation which can greatly upset the mother. Whilst many caring and loving new mothers are only too pleased to have their offspring removed to the nursery to enable them to get some rest, there are others who are very distressed by this separation. They are eager to see the fruits of their labour and feel also the need to continue without interruption the relationship which started months earlier. The taking away of the baby can also be seen as somewhat peremptory. So in order to avoid any misunderstanding, it is of enormous help if the views of the mothers on what is called 'rooming in' can be talked about in advance. Should there for any good medical reason be cause to separate mother and baby soon after the birth, it helps immensely if this is explained to the mother in a sensitive manner by the doctor or the midwife.

Severe depression must be regarded as a serious illness and needs immediate treatment, often with hospitalisation of the mother. There are, however, strong reasons for trying to avoid taking the mother away from her home environment even though she would of course be relieved of her responsibilities temporarily. Her feelings of inadequacy are likely to be increased when she sees that husband and baby can survive without her. Most important of all, the bonding of the mother with the baby is likely to be disrupted and this may be very difficult or even impossible to put right.

Irene Swyer has described some of the worst forms of post-natal depression as attributable to possible background factors:

Many factors may be involved in the causation of severe forms of post-natal depression. These go back to the early care of the mother herself; her relationship with her own mother; how wanted was *she*?; how much loving care did she have?; did she come from a home where there were both parents living a fulfilled life or was there strife, financial hardship, the children set against each other, one – perhaps her – made a scapegoat? Maybe she could have been an only child through whom the parents were trying to live their own lives and the burden had been too great for her. Perhaps the parents were split up or might have been dead. Her mother may have died in her very early childhood which could have created a great fear of her doing so herself prematurely. Her mother could even have died around the time of a sibling's arrival which could have predisposed her to dread the same thing happening to her.

Severe post-natal depression seems to have a close connection with poor early relationships, lack of verbal communication and maternal deprivation, where the new mother has so badly lacked good mothering. This often leads to a predisposition towards a depressive personality. Some people of this type find that big life changes such as changing schools or jobs, moving house, getting married and taking on full adult responsibilities, to say nothing of having a baby will make them very depressed. When a woman has her first baby she not only changes her role but she automatically changes the role of others. She becomes of course a mother, her husband a father and their parents may – unless there are other grandchildren – become grandparents for the first time. There are many who bitterly resent being relegated to grandparenthood and who openly express their views. For women with background factors such as these it is hardly surprising that pregnancy may evoke feelings of unease.

Of course, the world is not always like this. In contrast, those people who have had infertility problems and have been successfully treated by endocrinologists or other specialists, are usually ecstatic with joy when their babies arrive and, there is little doubt that they see their lives as being enriched by their new role.

WHC exists in order to help those who need advice and to help them to find a solution to their problems, if that is possible. Many such people think for a long time before they decide they must try to seek a possible answer. Sometimes, if a woman manages to see a psychotherapist whom she can grow to like and trust a firm relationship is built up between them with good result. Psychotherapists are not always easy to find and women, in particular, who have the right personal qualities and can undertake the necessary training to qualify in this skill, will always be a valuable asset in a society which indeed needs many more of them. In fact the future holds high promise if counsellors and psychotherapists can be employed in the Health Centres run by doctors which are described in the Conclusion to this book.

CHAPTER X

Sex and sexually transmitted diseases

For many people living in Western countries it was not until the 1950s and 1960s that sexuality became a topic of open discussion. Attitudes gradually changed then and a more frank, and a more permissive society emerged on the waves of popular publicity. Advances in the use of contraception not only gave couples better means of planning the size of their families but at the same time encouraged the development of a new kind of sexual freedom involving many in frequent changes of partner. Greater experimentation in sexual behaviour became widespread. For instance, the ancient practice of kissing partners' genitals (oral sex) had been regarded by most as unpleasant or embarrassing, but it is now a regular part of many people's activities. Some medical experts say however that, for the promiscuous, this has introduced another potential entrance into the body for viruses that have to be destroyed by the body's defence system against disease. There has in fact been an upward surge in the occurence of sexually transmitted diseases in both men and women and, although this may be nature's way of saying that everyone should be monogamous, it is doubtful whether the pendulum of behaviour will swing back that far when the next change of fashionable attitudes takes place.

Some people still hold the view that there should be no extra-marital sexual relationships. Their ancestors of two or three generations ago believed that both men and women should be discouraged from extra- or pre-marital sexual relations, yet many lives were complicated because men have tended to believe that they should have several partners while women were expected to have one. Some wives still try to turn a blind eye to this state of affairs – 'so long as he always comes home to me I don't want to know where or with whom he has been' – regardless of the possible risk to themselves of developing a sexually transmitted problem. Most of these husbands would take a different view if their wives behaved in the same way. The attitude projected in the 1960s suggested that many men and women would be expected to have a number of different partners during their lives. Many will forever disagree with this. There is no single 'correct' pattern for individual sexual behaviour and there never will be. It remains a personal decision and those who enjoy sex do not generally talk about it. It would be very boring for everyone else if they did!

Sexual intercourse between a man and a woman occurs after certain changes have taken place in their genital organs. Feelings of sexual desire originate in the mind and, in men, the penis fills with blood and causes an erection. In women blood flows to the walls of the vagina and 'lubricating liquid' is forced through the cells into the vaginal passage. Men often have an ever-ready sexual response which is generally maintained throughout most of their lives. They are most virile in their earlier years but they sometimes acquire sexual defects later on. They ejaculate (release semen containing sperms) into the vagina most times they have sexual intercourse and this is usually a pleasurable experience for them.

A man is unable to have intercourse unless his sexual response is complete and he has an erection. The situation is different for a woman. If her sexual response is not complete when the act takes place it is not pleasurable for her. Men who lack experience and understanding are often unaware of this. This is sometimes because the woman pretends to respond. The sex hormones in women fluctuate and change according to their monthly cycles (as explained in chapters VII and VIII) so that her response cannot always be reliable or complete. This is not to say that healthy women do not enjoy sex; but sometimes their enjoyment can increase in their middle and later years if they understand their own biological situation and it is managed with appropriate medical treatment when that is necessary.

There is a physical and mental rapport that makes sex desirable for both partners but if and when this is disrupted for any of the reasons – avoidable or unavoidable – that can damage emotions, one or other or both may be deeply upset. Heartbreak is as old as the hills and mending it means learning to live and perhaps to love again. Nothing is comparable with good sexual relations but sometimes the two people involved have little else in common. They may have different outlooks on life, interests and jobs, levels of intelligence and achievement, social habits, backgrounds or cultures and are sometimes years apart in age but they are brought together at some time in their lives through the physical attraction they have for each other. This situation may or may not last and all kinds of incompatibilities and reasons can cause individuals to want to find new partners or to convince themselves that friendship can mean more to them than sexual intercourse.

Treatment for psycho-sexual problems

Doctors are not always interested in treating psycho-sexual problems even though they deal with physical abnormalities. The Institute of Psycho-Sexual Medicine in London has been in existence since the early 1960s and it trains doctors already in general practice to deal with sexual problems. It will also supply the names of doctors to those who need professional counselling and care.

Most of the men and women who have asked Women's Health Concern to advise them have needed to talk to someone who can try to help them to overcome shyness, inhibitions and inadequacies. Women can be frigid and unable to relax with their partners. Men can lose confidence in themselves when they have failed to get an erection or they ejaculate too soon. There are many kinds of sexual 'hang-up'. Some of my African friends, who spent several years in Britain and other western countries in the 1970s studying for post-graduate degrees, have been genuinely shocked by the so-called sex-aids they saw in sex shops and they questioned their validity. They felt that our young people were being mis-informed by irresponsible perverts about sex and that there would be unfortunate consequences for some of them. Heterosexual practice is an essential and beautiful part of their own lives – and for most other people as well – but unless it comes 'naturally' they say it is not worth worrying about it.

For sex is surely a natural way of expression and it is mainly a non-verbal means of communication. It is so important to most people that it is one of the most discussed topics for both sexes at different times in their lives. Many have had harmless sexual fantasies in their young days but some fail to acknowledge such thoughts. This may have been because they were misled about themselves and their true feelings by damaging attitudes and values that were impressed upon them, or perhaps they enjoyed or deplored the 'dirty' jokes that so often amuse the public at large. Nevertheless many of them do try to take a serious view of the sexual side of their lives and there is now a wealth of good books about love-making and the different modes of sexual behaviour for people of all ages.

When the mutual desire is there the pleasures of sex start with getting to know one another and the exciting sensations they can develop in their minds and bodies as they grow closer together. Gently, and sometimes playfully, they touch and caress and kiss their partners in the areas that give them the most mutual pleasure. This is not just the erogenous areas – the breasts and the genitals – but the back of the neck, eyes that are closed and ears. Some of the ruinous experiences for young couples, who may become disillusioned with each other, can be caused by vigorous penile thrusting too soon by the man and pelvic movements by the woman that are too violent and quick. They can often wreck their chances of enjoying the subtle and loving moments between them that can postpone ejaculation and lead to much more pleasurable experience for both.

People vary in shape, size and temperament so much that each couple has to discover the positions in love-making that suit them best. They must get to know the right tempo for them and the extent of each one's sexual performance. Some women prefer to sit on top of the men because they find this is the easiest way for them to achieve an orgasm and to get breast stimulation. But there are a variety of other ways; him on top, side-by-side, both sitting up with her legs over his or he can enter her vagina from behind and put his arms around her to stimulate the clitoris. Digital stimulation, especially by her partner and sometimes by herself, during sexual intercourse can often add to the feelings of intense and utter pleasure that comes just before a woman has an orgasm and this usually increases their enjoyment. It is generally quicker for her to reach orgasm with clitoral stimulation by fingers rather than with the stimulation that can be achieved by sexual intercourse, but a woman usually finds the excitement of orgasm much greater with the penis inside her and this can be emotionally satisfying for her and for him too. When a woman is relaxed and happy and her pelvic muscles contract and release rythmically her mind can be relieved of all pressures – at least for the time-being – and the memories and the warm glow of the joys she has experienced can remain with her forever.

Homosexuals

Most people grow up knowing that they are male or female, and expecting to have families of their own at some future date, and during their adolescent years will have become conscious of the mutual attraction that exists between the sexes. Some people, however, find it difficult to accept the existence of men and women who look to persons of the same sex for their sexual satisfaction. Male homosexuals, and female homosexuals or lesbians, have always existed but in recent years they have become more generally accepted. Sometimes upsetting family experience or failure to respond sexually to the opposite sex is compensated by their homosexual activities which may prove to them that they are sexual after all. Others have been true homosexuals from the beginning. Their relationships can be lasting and sincere and give them personal satisfaction. Others, who enjoy a life-style that is free from any kind of personal commitment or family responsibilities, are often very promiscuous. Those who indulge also in drug-taking, and have contracted sexual diseases as well, are storing up immense problems for themselves and others (see pages 124–5).

Sexually transmitted diseases

Many of the recent inquiries to Women's Health Concern about sexually transmitted diseases come from people who fear they may have *herpes* (see pages 120–1). This is largely because since 1980 it has become a topic of wide discussion in the media. We advise inquirers to go to *special clinics* where they can be checked up and receive immediate medical attention. Some are found to have herpes infection – most of them not. One lady who suffers from multiple sclerosis was very upset when she discovered that her partner was sexually involved with other women and became concerned that she might develop herpes or some other sexual disease if she continued her relationship with him. Personal anxiety for themselves and their unborn babies is another worry for women who suffer recurring attacks of herpes. Some babies are delivered by caesarian section to avoid the risk of infection being passed on to them at birth (see page 121). Herpes infections, however – providing they are *properly monitored and managed* – are unlikely to lead to serious damage for either mothers or babies. Mental turmoil is suffered by those who fear they might pass their infection on to their partners. Herpes is spread by direct contact of the body surfaces and some recent work shows that the herpes virus can survive for a number of hours on a lavatory seat or on cotton gauze but that most infection results from direct sexual contact. There should be no sexual relations whatsoever when herpes attacks recur and no kissing when lip sores are present. Also herpes sufferers must remember to wash their hands after touching genital or mouth sores, especially after using the lavatory or applying creams to the sores. It is easy for them to infect other people and to reinfect themselves on another part of the body – eyes are particularly vulnerable.

Stresses between partners who have developed possible symptoms of sexual illness can be horrific – where did it come from – which one has been unfaithful? . . . A sexual illness is a very unpleasant experience.

Personal cleanliness

When making love both partners must pay full attention to their personal cleanliness. An important point for men to understand is that, if they have not been circumcised (circumcision is not medically essential), the foreskin must be pulled back every day and the penis carefully washed. Cancer of the penis may occur if this is neglected and there is a risk of their partners developing cancer of the neck of the womb because of constant irritation and inflammation of the genital passages.

Young women must also be warned that cancer of the womb (cervical cancer) is more prevalent in those who have had a number of sexual partners and in those who have started sexual intercourse at an early age.* There is plenty of evidence to show, for example, that this disease is common in prostitutes. Promiscuous sex can spread all kinds of infection.

Though medical know-how and treatment has provided satisfactory help for many who have suffered from known sexual diseases, a recent development has arisen in the form of a disease that is at present incurable – AIDS (see below page 124).

With the incidence of *syphilis* increasing also among homosexual men in large cities, the rise of promiscuity due to easy travel and the lessening of moral censure, no adult leading an active sex life is immune to such other diseases as *gonorrhoea* and lesser diseases like *non-specific urethritis*, *vulvo-vaginal infections*, *cystitis*, *thrush* and other common infections.

The WHC booklet *Sexually transmitted diseases* gives vital information for all men and women with an active sex life, whatever their age and inclinations.

Venereal disease

In the United Kingdom the words 'venereal disease' have a legal definition,

*See in Chapter V, about cervical smear tests, page 46.

because in 1917 an Act of Parliament was passed which specified three illnesses as the 'Venereal Disease': *syphilis, gonorrhoea* and an illness called *soft sore* or *chancroid*. This latter has now almost completely disappeared, though the other two, syphilis and gonorrhoea, remain very much with us.

Other sexually transmitted diseases include a wide range of infections caused by a variety of parasites, fungi, bacteria and viruses which are passed on by sexual contact.

There are a number of other conditions including *cystitis* and attacks of *vaginal thrush* which, though not actually transmitted during the act of intercourse, can be precipitated by it.

True venereal diseases differ from other sexually transmitted infections in three ways. Fifty or sixty years ago, these diseases were incurable and could have a serious effect on a patient's health. Furthermore, both could affect children and there was something especially unpleasant about the involvement of innocent victims with such diseases. Lastly, because of their mode of transmission, they were always associated with feelings of sexual guilt and morality. Nowadays most doctors in the United Kingdom tend, therefore, to reserve the words *veneral disease* strictly for those that are defined as such by the Act of Parliament and to use the simple name of the infection for other sexually transmitted disorders, a list of the more important of which is to be found in the table on page 126.

How these infections spread

It is very important for doctors to know what encourages the spread of these diseases since then they can attempt to control them, and ideally, to stop them spreading. Perhaps the two most important reasons for the spread of sexually transmitted diseases are promiscuous sexual behaviour and the presence in the community of a number of infected people. By sexual promiscuity we mean intercourse with more than one sexual partner and it is easy to see that if people were not promiscuous the diseases would be limited, even if infected people were among the community.

Conversely, if nobody in the community was infected, even though people behaved promiscuously there would be no spread of the disease. However, there is a lot of evidence to show that today the numbers of people infected with many of the sexually transmitted diseases and some of the venereal diseases are increasing and that a proportion of the population behaves in a sexually promiscuous manner. Consequently, this group of infections has shown noticeable increases over the past twenty-five years in nearly all parts of the world. Britain has been no exception, though as we have a specialised service to deal with the problem, the increase is less than that of other European countries and the United States.

Modern travel, enabling large numbers of people to move from country to country, on business and pleasure, has been another significant cause of the spread of these illnesses, and a further factor has undoubtedly been the revolution in birth control methods that has taken place over the past thirty years. The pill and intra-uterine device interpose no protective barrier between a couple having sexual relations, unlike the contraceptive sheath which also effectively prevents the transmission of germs from one partner to the other.

The incidence of venereal disease and other sexually transmitted diseases, in Britain today, can be assessed accurately since for several years Special Clinics throughout the country have kept records of the numbers of patients suffering from syphilis and gonorrhoea. From these we know that the numbers of cases of syphilis have fallen dramatically since the 1940s and that nowadays it is a fairly uncommon disease, though still present to a significant extent especially amongst homosexual men in large cities.

The problem of gonorrhoea is unfortunately quite different. This disease was at a high level at the end of the second world war but fell progressively until the early 1950s. Since then there has been a gradual increase until the 1970s during which the figures remained high, fluctuating a little from year to year. Nowadays it is a very common infection indeed, perhaps the most common in this country which can be cured with antibiotic treatment.

For the other sexually transmitted diseases detailed statistics have been collected for only a few years and are therefore of limited value but there is no doubt that many infections, and particularly *non-specific genital infections* in both men and women, have been increasing steadily year by year until they are now the commonest group of sexually transmitted diseases in the United Kingdom. There has also been a great increase of *genital herpes infections* over the past ten to fifteen years.

The provisions for dealing with sexually transmitted diseases in the United Kingdom

The Special Clinics

A number of clinics, usually one in every large hospital, were established throughout the country at the end of the first world war to deal with the large number of people suffering from syphilis and gonorrhoea. These clinics were usually known as Venereal Disease Clinics, though sometimes they are anonymous or had the name 'Special Clinic' to protect the feelings of patients who might go there, only to find that they were not suffering from the dreaded infections after all.

At these clinics doctors, nurses and social workers carry out the necessary technical tests. Nowadays, most but not all clinics have an appointment system. If someone is found to be infected with venereal disease, treatment is given and at an interview with a social worker an attempt is made to arrange for the partner or partners also to attend for tests.

After the end of the second world war there was some decline in the extent of gonorrhoea and syphilis, and the clinics became busier dealing with other problems such as *non-specific urethritis, herpes, thrush* and *vaginal discharge.* Nowadays, in many clinics much of the work is coping with such common female problems as vaginal thrush, cystitis, and most frequent of all, vaginal discharge.

The organisation of clinics varies from hospital to hospital. Most newly built clinics function in the out-patient departments. Most are now entitled 'Departments of Genito-Urinary Medicine', the new name for the speciality, which today deals with a much wider range of illnesses than formerly.

In a few clinics, patients are given numbers and their names are not used, but most units do use names though at the same time observing strict confidentiality. All hospital notes and data are confidential and are looked after by specially trained staff. However, all clinics have their own records as an additional security measure and these are not usually allowed out of the department.

The medical staff will not communicate with patients' doctors concerning their attendance at the unit without their permission, unless the doctor has referred them, though most patients do see that it is to their advantage for details of any illness to be sent to their GP.

The examinations and tests take only a few minutes and cause no pain or discomfort apart from the inevitable brief 'pinprick' of a blood test. Some results can be given at once and are generally enough to make a diagnosis or to reassure the patient that infection seems unlikely, though blood tests and other laboratory tests may take a day or two.

All in all, a visit to a clinic is not the ordeal people usually expect. The staff are generally friendly, quick, reassuring and non-censorious. They will help you if they can and if they can't they will refer you to someone else who can.

Syphilis

Syphilis, known colloquially by its old English name 'the pox' is undoubtedly the most serious of the two veneral diseases but today in Britain it is fortunately fairly rare, being found mainly in large cities and particularly among homosexual men.

It is caused by a small, corkscrew-shaped Treponema organism (it used to be called Spirochaeta) which is present in mouth, genital and skin lesions in those affected and is transmitted from patient to patient mostly during sexual intercourse. It can also spread during the early years of her infection from the mother's blood stream to her developing fetus which it may infect and indeed kill, by miscarriage or abortion. Alternatively, the infant may be born suffering from the disease.

Syphilis has a very long duration which is divided into well-defined stages, the infection persisting for twenty to thirty years during the whole of which time it may cause damage of one sort or another to those infected. In the early stages, within a few weeks of infection, a small sore appears at the original site of infection. This is usually on the genitals but it may be on the finger, lips, tongue, anus, breast or almost any part of the body which has been involved in close sexual contact. This ulcer, which may be of any size, is painless and tends to persist for a few weeks. It is highly infectious as its moist surface contains many of the organisms causing syphilis. But long before the ulcer appears the germs will have found their way into the blood stream and will have been distributed to every tissue in the body where they multiply and, in many people, eventually produce signs of their presence.

A few weeks or possibly months after the healing of the primary lesion, a generalised, non-irritating skin rash appears in a high percentage of those infected. This is known as the secondary stage of the disease and in many patients it is accompanied by general illness, such as fever, headache and a sore throat. However, probably as many as forty per cent of those infected do not develop these obvious signs of the disease. The skin rash of *secondary syphilis* eventually heals and the patient appears clinically well, entering into a period of latency where there are no signs or symptoms. At this stage the illness can only be detected by blood tests for syphilis, the best known of which is the *Wassermann Reaction (W.R.)* though this test is now old-fashioned and is often replaced by other, better tests. Despite their apparent well-being, in perhaps a third or more of all the patients infected, the germs of syphilis will be slowly causing damage to other tissues in the body, most importantly the heart, large blood vessels, the brain and central nervous sytem.

Syphilitic disease of the heart takes ten to fifteen years to develop and may eventually show itself by symptoms of heart failure, usually shortness of breath, which is the result in most cases of damage to one of the main heart valves. The treponemes can also damage the large blood vessels, especially the aorta causing a swelling (called an *aneurysm*) which eventually can burst with fatal results. When the central nervous system is damaged, attacks of *meningitis* can develop, or more seriously, the 'thinking' cells of the frontal cortex can be damaged so that the patient loses his ability to reason properly, becoming 'insane'. Seventy years or so ago this was a common fate of syphilitics whose condition usually progressed rapidly and ended in death in a few years, though nowadays this is extremely rare. The disease may attack the nervous system in other ways, leading to *paralysis, blindness* and other forms of *nervous disorder*, all nowadays thankfully very uncommon.

Syphilis has diminished rapidly since the beginning of this century. Partly this is due to better socio-economic conditions and education. But medicine has also helped by providing efficient weapons, firstly in the form of the blood test, which allows us to screen large numbers of patients and secondly the drug '606'. This was a compound of arsenic (so-called by its inventor, Paul Erhlich, because it was the 606th compound he tested before finding an effective one) and, although very toxic, it cured syphilis. It was introduced in the 1920s and was used until the late 1940s when it was replaced by *Penicillin* which was much more effective and almost totally non-toxic.

Congenital syphilis

One of the most unpleasant aspects of the two major venereal diseases is the risk of their transference to newborn children. Syphilitic women have a very high chance, particularly in the first two years of the infection, of passing on the illness to their developing babies. If the infection is severe, the child may die in the womb and be aborted. (Syphilis is one of the rare causes of abortion.) All pregnant women automatically have a blood test for syphilis as part of their ante-natal care and if infection is detected, prompt treatment can protect the fetus from syphilitic damage.

Treatment. The standard course is ten daily injections of Penicillin, extended to twenty-one daily injections if the nervous system is involved. The results are excellent and other drugs are available should patients become sensitive to Penicillin.

Gonorrhoea

This disease, colloquially known in this country as 'clap', is probably the most important of the sexually transmitted diseases and is certainly the commonest true venereal disease today. Its Greek name originated from a Roman physician, and comes from two words, one meaning 'seed' and the other 'to flow', because the main symptom was a discharge of secretion from the end of the penis and the ancients thought this discharge was seminal fluid. Accounts of gonorrhoea and of measures to prevent it appear in the bible in Leviticus.

The germ causing the disease, the *Gonococcus*, is a small, fragile, micro-organism which thrives only in conditions of warmth, moisture and low oxygen content. It is easily killed by drying, soap and water, or any antiseptic. It infects or gains a hold on only those parts of the body which are covered in wet skin called mucous membrane. Mucous membranes line the cavity of the mouth, the edges of the eyelid, the alimentary and the genital tracts. In men the water pipe (urethra) is the main site attacked in the genital area, while in women it is the neck of the womb (cervix) and the urethra. It can also affect the outer lips of the front passage (vagina) in female children who have not started their periods. When the periods begin, sex hormones cause the skin of the outer lips of the vagina to thicken and this thickening protects them against infection.

The gonorrhoea germ spreads from person to person by direct contact, in most cases during sexual intercourse. It can also spread by other contact: for instance, infected genital discharge may be transferred on the hands to the genitals of a partner, though this is rare: it may affect the eyes of a baby as a result of its passage down the birth canal of an infected mother; it may affect the throat and mouth as a result of oro-genital sexual practices. In homosexual men the disease may be present in the rectum (back passage), which is also a common place for the germ in women, where it seems to gain access to the delicate mucous membranes of the bowel from the vagina during the act of opening the bowels.

The incubation period (the time taken for the disease to gain a hold and produce symptoms) is variable, ranging from a few days to three weeks and it is important to notice that most infected women have no symptoms. Those that do may have some pain on passing water and have an increase in discharge, and occasionally both these symptoms can be present.

In men, the most important and usual symptom is a discharge from the penis, otherwise a most unusual symptom in a male. Because the urethra of the male is long (25 centimetres), a considerable amount of discharge is produced which attracts attention. In women the urethra is very short (2.5 centimetres) and the amount of secretion produced by infection is so small that it is rarely noticeable. This is one reason why women are often unaware that they are infected and the diagnosis of infection can be made only by testing samples from the urethra and the neck of the womb. An instrument called a speculum is inserted into the vagina to expose the neck of the womb and to enable specimens to be taken for laboratory examination. Women who have not been examined like this before may be afraid that it will be painful but in fact the carefully designed instrument, if properly used, will cause no discomfort and the examination and collection of specimens lasts less than two or three minutes. At the same time, the doctor will often take a smear from the neck of the womb for a 'cancer test'. The examination is usually concluded by an internal test to ensure that the ovaries, womb, etc. are normal and not inflamed.

A sample of pus from the penis can be stained and examined under the microscope very easily, and the germs of gonorrhoea can rapidly be identified by their shape. The same test is carried out on women from specimens taken from the urethra and the neck of the womb but it is less reliable than in the male because so many different germs live in the vagina of every healthy woman. They are harmless and most have their protective function of keeping the vagina acid and so discourage growth of harmful germs, but their presence makes it more difficult to detect the troublesome ones. So only about sixty per cent of women can have an accurate 'while you wait' microscopic diagnosis. It is essential to grow the germ in the laboratory, and the gonorrhoea germ is not the easiest to grow, though most big hospitals have such good facilities nowadays that diagnosis is very accurate.

To ensure that no infection is present in female patients, two negative sets of tests are necessary. One test gives about an eighty per cent accuracy and two tests bring it up to around ninety-five per cent, which is as accurate as possible in a biological test. Unfortunately, there is as yet no reliable blood test for gonorrhoea and research is being carried out to see whether such a time-saving test can be developed.

Most gonorrhoea patients come to no serious harm but there is always the risk of complications developing and such complications are more serious in women than in men. The germ may settle in Bartholin's gland, a small pea-sized gland at the lower end of the vagina, one on each side, within the lips. If the germs penetrate the gland they cause a large painful swelling. Other germs can also cause this problem and the commonest germ to do this is the organism which causes the ordinary boil (Staphylococcus).

The second complication is the one that makes gonorrhoea such a serious disease for women. This is when the germs spread through the womb to infect the Fallopian tubes, a condition known as *salpingitis* or *pelvic inflammatory disease.* When salpingitis develops it causes a pain low down in the abdomen, usually on both sides, colicky or like a period pain, and it may range from mild to severe, closely immitating appendicitis and difficult to diagnose. The sad thing about pelvic inflammatory disease, apart from the fact that it may cause long-lasting pelvic discomfort, is that a high percentage of those affected by it become infertile because blocked tubes prevent the passage of the egg from the ovary to the uterus. This most important aspect of gonorrhoea underlines the fact that the possibility of gonococcal infection in a woman must always be taken very seriously.

Gonorrhoea in pregnant women

If a woman has gonorrhoea, her baby's eyes may be infected with the germ during passage through the neck of the womb when it is born. This usually shows within a day or two of birth as an acute inflammation of the eyes, which attracts immediate attention. Nowadays it is easily cured by antibiotics but years ago it often led to loss of sight.

Gonococcal complications in the male

Before effective treatment was readily available infection in the urethra could lead to scarring, resulting in narrowing and partial obstruction and making urination difficult and painful. Treatment of urethral stricture consists of the passage of graduated dilators through the urethra to stretch it, a procedure which requires skill, causes discomfort, risks further infection and has to be repeated from time to time.

Another possible consequence of delayed or ineffective treatment is the passage of germs along the ducts entering the urethra from the testicles. The first part of these ducts is a fine, coiled tube about twenty feet long called the *epididymis*, which is attached to the back of the testis. It continues as the *vas deferens* to open into the urethra. Gonococci travelling up these tubes can set up inflammation which causes pain and swelling of the testicle, and when this subsides leaves a blockage of the epididymal duct. Total sterility results if both sides are blocked and though a delicate operation to short-circuit the blockage (vaso-epididymostomy) may overcome the obstruction, its success rate is not high, even in the most skilled hands.

Disseminated Gonococcal Infection

When gonorrhoea remains undetected for a long time, the organism may find its way into the blood stream and be disseminated to the skin and joints, producing an illness characterised by fever, pains in the joints (particularly ankles, wrists and shoulder) and the appearance in the skin of scattered, scanty, reddish spots. Patients are not very ill and are often treated with antibiotics and cured, without the doctor or indeed the patient, even suspecting the true diagnosis. Because this condition tends to affect those who have had the disease without symptoms, it is particularly common in women and in homosexual men with gonoccal infection of the rectum. Very rarely, gonococci can gain access to a joint, particularly the ankle, wrist or knee, and produce a very severe infection which, if not treated rapidly, can seriously damage the lining of the joint.

The management and treatment of Gonorrhoea

In this country the treatment of gonorrhoea is still simple and straightforward, most of the strains responding rapidly to treatment with either a single injection of penicillin or by pencillin tablets. In other parts of the world, particularly Africa and the Far East, many gonococcal organisms have become relatively resistant to penicillin and infections acquired in these areas are usually treated with one of a wide variety of other, more expensive though equally effective antibiotics. Such infections do not prove a problem to manage in the relatively affluent Western societies but in many parts of the developing world, where money, doctors and drugs are in short supply, this change in the behaviour of gonococcus is a most serious one for the public health. An even more serious form of penicillin resistance has developed where the gonococcal germ produces an enzyme which destroys penicillin, making the organism completely resistant to penicillin no matter how much is administered. Once again, this strain of germ seems to have originated in the Far East and Africa, but it is now widely spread throughout Europe and is present in the United Kingdom. In reasonably affluent societies this presents no problem as other antibiotics are available which can cure the disease, but in the Third World, where money is a serious problem, these alternative antibiotics are too expensive.

After treatment has been completed it is essential for tests to be carried out to prove that the germ of gonorrhoea has been eliminated, especially in women. Most hospitals insist on a minimum of two tests.

To summarise, gonorrhoea is a common infectious disease which displays few symptoms of its presence in women. Men usually develop a discharge from the penis and quickly seek treatment. But although the disease is without symptoms in the majority of women, their grave risk is infertility. Men may also become sterile through blockage of the sperm ducts by gonococcal inflammation. Treatment in the West is simple, cheap and painless. The doctor who treats a patient with gonorrhoea should do

111

his best to persuade the patient to bring his or her partner along so that they too may be treated.

Non-specific Urethritis (NSU)

This condition presents itself almost solely in men because it does not cause recognisable symptoms in women. There is a thin discharge of pus from the penis caused by infection of the urethra. It is called 'non-specific' because, when it was first recognised, the cause of the infection was unknown. We now know that there is certainly more than one cause and others remain to be identified, so the name has been retained. The condition also exists in women but, because of the very short length of the female urethra, it produces few symptoms or signs. In the female the infection seems to be present mainly in the neck of the womb, which is a common site for mild infections and once again it can go unnoticed by the patient.

The condition is transmitted during sexual intercourse and has an incubation period of ten to twenty days though as the symptoms are so slight this incubation period may sometimes apparently extend for many weeks. Male patients may complain of a little discomfort on passing urine and the presence of a little discharge at the end of the penis, this being particularly noticeable when passing the first urine of the day. Sometimes the discharge may be more profuse.

If untreated, it may persist for many weeks or months and will eventually heal without serious trouble. In a small proportion of patients, it may track up from the urethra to damage the epididymis. In probably less than one per cent of all those infected, the disease can be associated with inflammation of the joints and eyes, a condition known as *Reiter's Disease*.

Diagnosis is made by taking a sample of the pus and trying to detect gonorrhoea germs. If they are not found, a diagnosis of non-specific urethritis is made, backed up by a further attempt to see if gonorrhoea germs can be cultured in the laboratory. If the cultures are negative, the diagnosis of non-specific urethritis is confirmed.

Treatment is by appropriate antibiotics, which are given by mouth, usually for a minimum of two weeks. Well over eighty per cent of patients are completely cured, though there can be recurrence in some men. Long-term effects rarely develop.

Non-specific Urethritis in women

Diagnosis in women can rarely be made by a doctor as a result of his examination or tests. What usually happens is that if a woman's partner is found to have non-specific urethritis, her doctor usually assumes that she has it too, after examination has excluded the presence of other logical genital diseases. She will usually have few, if any, signs of the disorder and there will very rarely be any significant clinical symptoms.

It is important that she should receive treatment because she may reinfect her partner, and there is also a slight but definite risk that one of the major causes of non-specific urethritis could produce an infection of a new-born baby's eyes. This infection is not usually serious but it can be troublesome. It has also recently been shown that the infection may produce a pneumonia in the new-born child. Some doctors believe that there is a risk of the infection spreading to involve the Fallopian tubes but the extent of this risk is not yet known. Unfortunately, as so few women have any symptoms of this disease, it is common for them to receive no treatment even after seeking medical advice.

It is now clear that about half the cases of NSU are due to an organism called *Chlamydia trachomatis.* This strange organism cannot be grown on an artificial culture medium but reproduces only inside living cells. In hot, dry parts of the world it spreads from person to person to infect the eyes, producing *trachoma.* With inadequate treatment this disease can cause scarring of the eye and blindness, but this never happens in this country to babies infected during birth. In cooler, more developed parts of the world, where doctors and drugs abound, it has adopted a sexual mode of transmission and appears to be the major cause of NSU. All the same, in at least forty per cent of the cases of NSU the cause has not yet been identified.

There are a number of other mysteries about non-specific urethritis because, while it is certainly commoner in men and women who lead sexually promiscuous lives, it can turn up in a sexual partnership where neither partner has been unfaithful to the other. This usually happens after childbirth, the insertion of an intra-uterine coil and so on, when it seems probable that outside germs have been introduced or the local germ population in the genital tract has temporarily increased to cause an infection in the partner.

Briefly then, non-specific urethritis is the commonest of all sexually transmitted diseases and the doctor's main job used to be to ensure the patient's infection was not a gonococcal one. Probably today, his most important task is to ensure that the female partner, who will often have no symptoms, receives full treatment. Over all, the response to treatment is good and with the exception of pelvic inflammatory disease, serious complications are unusual.

Evidence increasingly points to the likelihood that today in the Western world, chlamydial infections may be a more important cause of pelvic inflammatory disease than gonococcal infections.

VULVO-VAGINAL INFECTIONS AND CYSTITIS

The vulva and vagina are areas which, for a number of reasons, are extremely prone to infection. The vagina (the internal passage leading to the womb) is about four inches long. Its walls normally touch each other. It continues from the womb to the outside where it is continuous with the inner and outer lips of the vulva. Above the vagina is the opening of the urethra, from which urine is passed and this is surmounted by the clitoris and its hood. Below the vaginal opening is the anus or back passage and this area is always a possible source of infection.

The vagina is normally kept healthy by a delicately balanced system of effects produced by micro-organisms which live in the vagina. These produce substances which accurately adjust the level of acidity so that it supports only harmless or beneficial organisms.

Other important factors are the sex hormones which influence the thickness of the lining and also cause the production of a sugar in the cells of the lining. This sugar is essential to a group of normal bacteria which live in the vagina and ferment the sugar, producing chemicals which maintain the degree of acidity at such a level as to make it difficult for disease-causing germs to grow.

Other factors can unfavourably affect the acid safety margin in the vagina, such as the flow of alkaline mucus from the neck of the womb, which normally takes place in the middle of the cycle at ovulation, (though at this time the acidity of the vaginal secretions is greatest) and the flow of alkaline blood during menstruation. During the menstrual period, therefore, infections of the vagina are more likely.

The delicate balance of the vagina can easily be tipped in favour of infection in other ways and it is important to stress here the risks of contamination after opening of the bowels. If toilet tissue is used and the anus is wiped from behind to forward, faecal matter and bacteria can easily be deposited on the vulva. The anus should therefore always be wiped with a single stroke from front to back and a fresh tissue used for each wipe. Ideally, the area should be washed afterwards.

When antibiotics are used, to cure a sore throat or pneumonia, for example, they can also kill the protective germs in the vagina. As a result of this, germs insensitive to the antibiotics may 'take over' the vagina, and produce a clinical infection. A good example of this is *vaginal thrush*. But, without doubt, one of the commonest causes of vaginal infection is the introduction of germs by sexual intercourse, when three things may happen. First the male may have germs on his penis, either the agents of sexually transmitted disease or venereal disease, or normal germs, present in large amounts. When a woman responds sexually, the lubrication produced in the vagina is an alkaline liquid as is the seminal fluid ejaculated by the man into the vagina. Thirdly, during intercourse, minor damage can take place to the lining of the vagina and thus for four to six hours after intercourse, conditions favour the development of infections.

Another thing to remember about *vulvo-vaginal infections* is that the vagina contains little in the way of sensory nerve endings so that infections there tend to cause no symptoms and it is not until they affect the vulva that symptoms of itching, burning or pain are experienced, particularly after passing urine.

Most women nowadays are aware of the need to pay attention to the hygiene of the vulva. However, many young women are unaware of the fact that to ensure absolute cleanliness and freedom from infection, daily washing should include separation of the narrow gap between the inner lips of the vulva, particularly where they run together over the clitoris. This should be carefully washed every day with a soft flannel and soap. There are two small glands by the clitoris which produce a form of sweat called *smegma* and if this is not washed away daily, smegma can sometimes build up into yellowish material and also cause irritation.

A word about vaginal odours may not be out of place here. The first point to appreciate is that the genitals smell. The odour of the vulval area in a healthy woman is a mildly 'fishy' smell. The same thing is also true of the male and it is probable that this odour was at one time a powerful sexual attractant. Indeed it still is to many people today. If infection of the vulva and the vagina are present, an unpleasant smell may develop. This has often been compared to the smell of boiling greens and it is the smell of pus wherever it is formed in the body. Some women notice an accentuation of vaginal odour around menstruation but this is normal. Vaginal deodorant sprays are unnecessary for healthy women. An unacceptable vaginal smell always means that infection is present. In this connection, one very common cause of offensive vaginal discharge is a forgotten menstrual tampon which should always be looked for in such circumstances.

Careful daily washing of the vulva also provides an opportunity to notice spots, lumps or lesions and advice about the nature of these can quickly be sought.

The vulva is like any other part of the body in that it varies from person to person but women do not have the same opportunity as men to compare their genitals with each other. Many women believe that they are abnormal because of a difference in size, say between the two inner lips of the vulva, but this is a very common variation and there are many others, particularly in the size, shape and even position of the clitoris. If a woman feels concerned about this, she should ask her doctor for reassurance.

Ideally, the vulva should be kept dry but this ideal is not helped by modern fashions in underwear and the fabric from which garments are made. For example, tight, closely fitting nylon pants do not allow perspiration to evaporate as do cotton pants, and this is often made worse by wearing a second layer of tightly fitting nylon tights on top. Old-fashioned stockings and suspenders, or modern open-crotch tights, are preferable for vulval health. Overweight women have difficulty in keeping the vulva dry, and constant dampness can lead to irritation and dermatitis.

Vaginal discharge

As it has been said that nearly every woman complains of vaginal discharge at some time or other, it would be a good idea to consider what is normal. Some discharge from the vagina is common just before the onset and after the completion of menstruation. This sometimes causes anxiety in young girls but there is no need for alarm. When, in the middle of a cycle, ovulation takes place, clear, sticky mucus is produced by the glands in the neck of the womb. It may take a few days for this secretion to be discharged and when it does it may 'come away' in quite a large amount, rather like the egg white of a partially boiled egg. This normal mucus produces a pale, honey-coloured stain when dry, whereas discharge resulting from infection always produces a yellowish or greenish stain.

Discharge from the vagina during sexual activity is normal and many women notice an increase in secretion when they start taking the contraceptive pill. Apart from this a discharge for a woman is abnormal if it is something she does not normally get, if it has an offensive smell, if it is so copious that it soaks her underwear and causes her trouble, or if it persistently produces a yellowish or greenish stains on her underwear. Blood-stained discharge is particularly important after the menopause and always requires investigation. At other times, occasional blood-stained discharge is usually of no special significance but advice should always be sought if it persists.

Vaginal Thrush

Vaginal Thrush, which is caused by a yeast, usually Candida albicans, has become one of the commonest causes of *vulvo-vaginitis* in sexually active women, especially in the last fifteen to twenty years. The reasons for this may have something to do with the widespread use of antibiotic drugs, as well possibly with the increase in promiscuous sexual activity over the past twenty years. The first thing to appreciate is that the thrush yeast can be found on normal skin and in the normal vagina, without causing any trouble. In certain conditions, however, it becomes aggressive and causes a local infection. Minor trauma which damages the delicate vaginal lining is common during sexual intercourse and this often allows thrush to get a hold. Increased sugar levels in diabetic women allow the yeast to cause infection and the same thing can happen in pregnancy for the same reason. In severe general diseases thrush can infect many body cavities and be a serious problem. Thrush infections often seem to develop after the patient has received a course of antibiotics, presumably because these medicines kill the normal vaginal organisms but leave the thrush untouched.

The main symptoms of thrush are vaginal discharge and, most of all, itching and burning. Sexual intercourse is painful and leaves an unpleasant aching, burning feeling. Urine passed over the sore and inflamed skin can burn so that a mistaken diagnosis of *cystitis* can easily be made by both patient and doctor. The discharge ranges from a typical greyish-white, curdy secretion (like yoghourt), to a thin yellow one. There is a tendency for the infection to wax and wane, clearing up before a period but returning around the time of menstruation.

If left untreated, thrush can spread to the skin of the outer lips of the vulva and the thigh. Diagnosis is usually easy but it should always be confirmed with the proof of a swab test. There are many causes of vaginal itching, and thrush, though the commonest, is only one of them.

Treatment is simple and straightforward for the great majority of cases, consisting of the insertion of a pessary into the vagina each night and the application of cream to the skin of the vulva twice daily for as long as directed by the doctor, depending upon the preparation prescribed. Treatment should always be continued throughout menstruation. In general it is not necessary to stop sexual relations after the first few days of treatment.

This cures most women but about a third have relapses, particularly around menstruation, which require further treatment. When incompletely cured, the itch and discharge go but pain at intercourse persists. Further tests have to be made to establish whether or not the yeast is still present and if it is, further treatment is required. If not, there may be other causes for the continuing pain which will need appropriate treatment. If not dealt with, pain on intercourse can persist and develop into a major problem threatening the stability of a sexual partnership.

Men get thrush on the genitals, nearly always by sexual transference. It produces an itchy, burning, red, spotty inflammation on the end of the penis and foreskin. As with some women, some men appear to be particularly susceptible to thrush infection which may develop after every episode of sexual intercourse and can prove very troublesome. But provided that there is no underlying predisposing disease such as diabetes, genital thrush in men is easily and quickly treated by the local application of fungicidal cream to the affected area.

Trichomoniasis

This is the name given to infestation of the vagina and the urethra by a small, pear-shaped parasite called *Trichomonas vaginalis*. In most cases it is transferred by sexual intercourse but babies can occasionally be infected from their mothers. There are two main symptoms, the commonest being a profuse, irritating, yellowish and smelly vaginal discharge. The second symptom, which does not occur in all patients, results from involvement of the urethra, causing burning and increased frequency of passing urine. The discharge can be so profuse that underwear is soaked and the skin of the thighs becomes reddened and inflamed. Fortunately, diagnosis is simple by examining a sample of the vaginal secretions under the microscope.

Men may also suffer from this condition, which causes an attack of *urethritis* or burning and frequency of passing urine. Unfortunately in the majority of men infected with this parasite, symptoms are absent so the man can act as a 'carrier'. It is therefore an accepted practice that when a woman is found to have this infection, her male partner is always offered treatment even though he may have no symptoms. If this is not done, it is likely that the woman will relapse repeatedly.

Treatment is simple. The drug *Flagyl* is given by mouth for a week in a fairly low dosage, or for twenty-four or forty-eight hours in a higher dosage.

The important thing about *trichomoniasis* from the doctor's point of view is that it alerts him to the possibility of other sexually transmitted infections and tests for these should always be made. The disease has no long-term consequences.

Cystitis

Cystitis technically means an inflammation of the bladder while *urethritis* means an inflammation of the tube leading from the bladder to the outside. In women, cystitis is an extremely common complaint from babyhood to old age and this is due to the fact that the distance from the outside of the skin to the lining of the bladder is very short in women. The outside skin can easily be contaminated by germs from the bowel and these are the ones that usually cause attacks of cystitis.

In the male, cystitis is very uncommon and when it occurs is usually due either to a germ caught during sexual intercourse or to the presence of some underlying abnormality of the urinary tract. The reasons for the male's relative freedom are the length of the male urethra, and the fact that it does not end on skin which can easily be contaminated with germs.

The symptoms of cystitis are a burning pain on passing urine, experienced most commonly towards the end of the act, and increased frequency of urination. In severe cases, the bladder is so inflamed that bleeding occurs and the urine is bloodstained. Cystitis is more common in sexually active women and many find that their attacks of cystitis can be related to intercourse. Others find that attacks are connected with their menstrual periods, for there is no doubt that female hormone levels affect the urinary tract of women just as they do the vagina. Some women find cold weather or even particular foods seem to precipitate attacks, while others can find no predisposing causes.

There are probably two reasons why sexual intercourse causes attacks of cystitis. Germs from the outside may be introduced during the act of sex and the urethra runs in the front wall of the vagina. In some women the opening of the urethra may be quite low, virtually in the vagina, and therefore subject to trauma during intercourse. Germs can almost be pushed into the urethra.

To prevent cystitis being caused by sexual intercourse there are some useful tips. Always keep the vulval and perianal areas scrupulously clean. It is a wise precaution always to pass urine after sexual intercourse to ensure that any germs which may have been pushed into the urethra have a good chance of being rinsed away by the flow of urine. If they are not and the woman does not pass urine for say, seven or eight hours, there is ample opportunity for the germs to multiply rapidly. If these simple tips do not help, a single tablet of a sulphonamide, an antibiotic or some other drug that will inhibit the growth of the germs causing cystitis should be taken before sexual intercourse for a few weeks.

Patients and doctors do not always agree about what constitutes cystitis. From the doctor's point of view, a diagnosis can only be made accurately when a specific germ, known to be capable of infecting the bladder, is grown in the laboratory in significant numbers from a sample of the patient's urine. Very often, the patient may have the symptoms of cystitis yet laboratory tests show no evidence of infection. This collection of symptoms is common and is called 'the urethral syndrome'. It is suspected that such infection is confined to the urethra, which gives the patients symptoms of frequency and burning, yet is not sufficient to produce positive laboratory results in the bladder urine. Some patients with this form of disorder will go on to develop full-blown cystitis but the great majority recover within a few days without antibiotics though persistence and recurrence can be troublesome. It seems to be a peculiar feature of urinary-tract infection in both sexes that the pain produced by the infection is so intense that the mind seems to 'remember' the pain. Equally, the prospect of having to go and pass urine where there are no proper facilities makes many of us anxious, and one of the commonest symptoms of anxiety is an increased desire to pass water. These points are important because in many cases of 'cystitis' without infection of the bladder, the symptoms are genuine but they require different handling and are unlikely to be cured by an antibiotic alone.

A small percentage of recurrent cases of cystitis in both sexes may be the result of an underlying disease or abnormality of the bladder or kidneys. Patients with this pattern of illness should always be investigated by a specialist urologist. What happens here is that first of all samples of the urine are taken as usual for examination in the laboratory. Then an X-ray of the kidneys called an *intravenous pyelogram* or *IVP* will be performed to show the outline of the kidneys and main urinary passages. Depending on the findings, the urologist may carry out a *cystoscopy* in which a small telescope is inserted through the urethra into the bladder so that he can examine it.

VIRAL SEXUALLY TRANSMITTED DISEASES

Herpes is an extremely common infection, familiar to most people as 'cold sores'. The Type I virus is mild, affects the mouth and lips, and is generally transmitted from person to person by close bodily contact, especially kissing. Most adults over the age of twenty-one will either have had a history of infection or will have had attacks even through they may have been so slight as to have remained unnoticed. They nevertheless will have left behind some immunity. The other strain, Type II, mainly affecting the genitals and spread by sexual relations, is often accompanied by other sexually transmitted diseases. This is a much more unpleasant virus and can cause one of the most painful and distressing sexually transmitted disorders for a woman.

The behaviour of the virus is remarkable. As soon as it penetrates the mucous membranes of the mouth or genitals it finds a nerve fibre along which it travels rapidly to a collection of ganglion cells just outside the spinal cord and there it survives for the rest of the person's life. The virus lives in a collection of nerve cells near the brain in the case of oral strains and in a collection of nerve cells at the end of the spine in the case of genital infections. Meanwhile, where the virus first entered, an attack of herpes will produce a group of burning, itchy little blisters which rapidly burst to produce a number of shallow ulcers. Because they expose the nerve endings, these ulcers are extremely painful, especially for women when urinating. In first attacks of the disease there may be headache, raised temperature, backache and a general feeling of illness. Often, passing urine may be so difficult that the patient has to be admitted to a hospital for a day or so.

A variety of treatments is available to help the pain and to speed up the process of healing but there is no actual 'cure' for this infection in the sense that the virus living in the nerve ganglia can be destroyed. A new and very important drug called 'Acyclovir' has been developed which is capable of preventing the virus of herpes from reproducing itself and it is rapidly effective in attacks of herpetic infection when taken by mouth or applied locally in a cream. This drug is, unfortunately, very expensive. It does not prevent recurrences though it lessens their severity. Recurrences are seen in fifty or eighty per cent of patients as from time to time the virus comes down nerve fibres and arrives in the mouth or genitals, causing an attack.

Patients often find that it follows sexual intercourse or, in the case of oral herpes, exposure to sunshine or at the time of a cold or menstruation. As oro-genital sexual practices are now common Type I strain herpes virus is frequently transferred from the mouth to the genitals to produce a similar attack of genital herpes to a Type II strain, though a little less severe. A vaccine is also under investigation which may prevent infection in those who have not yet met the virus and may also be helpful in cutting down or preventing recurrence. It is not yet fully tested nor generally available.

Patients may sometimes be surprised to discover that they have herpes when their partner has no gential or oral lesion, which illustrates one of the problems of herpes infections, that they can be transmitted unnoticed by anyone who has had the disease. In fact, most cases of genital herpes are acquired from partners who do not have obvious lesions of the mouth or genitals at the time of sexual contact. From time to time, anyone who has had a herpes infection – and it should be stressed that eighty per cent or more of the adult population will have had one – will secrete virus in the genital or salivary secretions and could infect someone who has not had the disease by genital or oral contact.

Research has shown that in some way and in some patients, herpes Type II infections of the cervix appear to be associated with the later development of *cancer of the cervix.* But the precise nature of this association is not yet clear. This certainly does not imply that anyone with genital herpes will develop cancer of the cervix. Hundreds of thousands of people get herpes without developing cancer, so other factors are involved. Nevertheless many doctors consider it a wise precaution for any girl who has had genital herpes to have a yearly cancer smear as long as the precise connection between herpes and cancer of the cervix remains uncertain. After all, this happens to be the one cancer in the body which can be detected by cancer smear tests years before it is fully developed. Many doctors now feel that other infectious agents, particularly viruses that may affect the genitals, could play a part in the development of cervical cancer and much research into these possibilities is being undertaken.

There are a number of other special problems concerning herpes infection in women and the first of these is the danger of the illness in the newly born child. Herpes in newly born infants is a very serious condition indeed and the risk to babies is that, if the mother has active herpetic sores present in the genital tract during the time the baby is being born, there is a serious risk of herpetic infection. In such circumstances, a Caesarian section is usually performed, which reduces the risk that the child will be infected. Women who have had genital herpes should always inform their obstetrician and today in most hospitals swabs for virus will be taken at weekly intervals towards the end of the pregnancy and if a positive result is obtained, the question of a Caesarian birth will be seriously considered. It should be remembered that fortunately, in this country, herpes in infants is extremely rare.

Those who find their disease difficult to cope with for a variety of reasons, may be able to solve their problems by joining one of the support groups, founded for this purpose such as the Herpes Association.

Genital warts

The common wart which occurs on the skin of the feet and hands is also due to a virus. A slight variation of this virus is often sexually transmitted and produces warts on the skin, particularly the mucous membrane of the genital area, which can be extremely troublesome. The incubation period ranges from a few weeks to many months and the number of warts produced in an individual ranges from one or two to hundreds forming large masses that can even reach the size of a small orange. Mostly, however, they show as small, firm, slightly gritty, irregular tongue-like projections of tissue about the size of a match-head. Sometimes they collect in little plaques of tissue, rather like a cauliflower in appearance, and these can range from a few to masses as big as a thumbnail. They occur anywhere on the genitals – in the vagina, on the cervix and, in both sexes, around the opening of the anus. They hardly ever occur on the skin of the thighs. They are troublesome to treat, largely because of their sensitive site, but would be easy enough to manage in hospital, under an anaesthetic by electro-cautery, a simple operation taking only a few minutes. Such treatment is usually reserved for really troublesome warts or for patients with very large collections of these irritating tumours. Most respond well to regular application of caustic substances but this has to be carried out by a doctor or a nurse because if applied in error to normal skin, it can cause serious burns.

It has now been appreciated that genital wart virus often infects the cells of the cervix and whilst this may sometimes produce warts which are visible to the naked eye, it often produces changes which may only be evident when a 'pap' smear (cancer smear) is taken. These changes, whilst not showing evidence of cancer, may alarm the pathologist and he will have to order a series of repeat smears until the changes return to normal. Examination of the neck of the cervix with a magnifying apparatus (colposcope) has made it easy to identify these areas of wart infection and many doctors believe that all women with vulval warts should have a colposcopy to ensure the cervix is free from viral infection. If any of the viral lesions are found, they can easily be destroyed by the electric cautery, the cold cautery or by a laser.

Parasitic infections

Pubic Lice (Pediculosis pubis) is due to infestation of the hair of the genital and sometimes perianal regions by a human body louse. This louse has very prominent pincer-like feet to enable it to hold on to hair and is named the crab louse. It can spread to other areas of the body but never appears on the hair of the head. In the great majority of cases it is transferred by the close contact of sexual relations, but it can also be acquired from infested bedding and, very occasionally, even from lavatory seats. The creatures bite and feed on the blood of their victims which causes intense local irritation and small reddish spots on the pubic skin. The insects themselves are brownish-grey, about the size of a pin-head, and lay eggs which are fastened by a glue to the base of the hairs. As the hairs grow, these eggs or 'nits' are found further away from the base of the hair.

Treatment is easy, involving the application of an appropriate shampoo, cream or lotion to the infected areas. There is no need for the hair to be shaved.

Scabies

This infestation, due to an itch mite, is usually transmitted by non-sexual contact but can also be acquired sexually, in which case the earliest signs tend to appear on the genitals. The mite burrows in the skin and lays its eggs there. This causes intense irritation and thus the symptoms of scabies are the appearance at the original site of infection of a number of little papules which are intensely itchy. When sexually transmitted these signs usually appear on the penis, scrotum, vulva or skin of the thighs. Though it is rather rare to find scabies in the vulval area, the disease frequently spreads to involve all the skin of the body and a prominent symptom is generalised itching, particularly while in bed at night when the body is warm.

Treatment again is fairly simple, involving the application of a lotion which has to be applied on at least two separate occasions and it is essential that possibly infected bed-linen and underclothing are changed after the first treatment. In a household, it is usual to find that all the family are infected and all will usually require treatment.

Common minor abnormalities of the genital area
In men, the hair follicles of the penis and scrotum are very prominent, due to the fact that the skin in these sites is much thinner than elsewhere in the body. These hair follicles appear as small, firm, visible tiny nodules about half the size of the head of a match, which can also be felt as little gritty lumps. They are often noticed for the first time by young men during adolescence, causing a great deal of worry.

In women, the skin of the vulva may present a similar appearance due to the hair follicles and sebaceous glands. Sometimes these small glands swell up to produce a bigger yellowish swelling, three or four millimetres in diameter, which may look quite alarming. These too need cause no concern as they soon settle down and disappear.

'Boils' are infections of hair follicles and are common in those parts of the body where there is perspiration and hair, such as the genital areas, pubic region and perianal areas. It is a strange thing that a boil on the arm causes no alarm but the same lesion in the genital region will produce an immense amount of anxiety. A special variety of boils, which are sometimes seen in the genital area and other parts of the body, results when sebaceous glands, of which there are many in the skin in this region, become infected and produce rather larger, swollen, red, tender swellings which may break down to discharge a mixture of purulent secretion and yellowish sebaceous material.

Haemophilus or Gardnerella Vaginalis Vaginitis
This extremely common condition was recognised over forty years ago but it is only in recent years that doctors have begun to realize how common it is and to consider it as an illness in its own right.

The common symptoms it produces are of a very strong scanty but malodorous discharge with a strong ammoniacal/fishy smell. This smell is usually much more noticeable after sexual relations and the reason for this is that alkaline male sperm releases some strongly smelling chemicals from the organisms and the cells they infect.

Treatment is not very satisfactory in that although symptoms may be rapidly relieved by the drug Flagyl or certain antibacterial creams, relapse in some people is very common. Whether or not the illness is connected with a similar infection in the male, is debatable. Some authorities say that men are infected with this organism whilst others, although admitting that this infection can take place, find it to be a fairly rare happening. It appears to have no serious consequences.

AIDS

AIDS stands for *'acquired immune deficiency syndrome'*. It seems to be a new disease complex which appeared initially amongst homosexual men resident in Los Angeles and New York in the 1970s. The disease is characterised by a paralysis of the body's immune defences which in itself produces no symptoms for the affected patient. This immune paralysis can be detected, if it is suspected, by very sophisticated and expensive laboratory tests. A number of men with these abnormalities go on to develop a mild form of illness where they feel generally unwell, lose weight and develop enlarged lymphatic glands which are found throughout the body. Mild diarrhoea and indigestion may also be associated.

The main syndrome usually develops when the patient is taken seriously ill with one of a number of different so-called 'opportunistic' infections. These infections do not normally attack healthy people and are generally only seen in those who are terminally ill or in whom their immune systems have been paralysed, either by disease or by treatment. (A temporary and partial paralysis of the body's immune machinery is often part of the necessary treatment following an organ transplant. This is to prevent the body from rejecting the transplanted organ.)

These illnesses take a wide variety of forms but the most serious is a pneumonia caused by a germ called *Pneumocystis carinii.* Candida albicans, herpes infections and a number of illnesses often seen only in animals, can develop. In a number of patients, these illnesses prove fatal. Another group of men suffering from the disease go on to develop what was previously a rare form of cancer known as *Kaposi's sarcoma.* This too, usually proves to be fatal. It is thought that the cancer develops because the immune system is no longer working properly and is not able to do its job of detecting abnormal cells when they arise in the body and then destroying them. Cancers in other parts of the body have been reported in patients with AIDS.

AIDS has now been reported in some heterosexual women, intravenous drug users and patients who have received multiple blood transfusions. This was first noticed amongst haemophilia sufferers. Some babies born to mothers with AIDS have themselves developed the illness. The final group of patients have been immigrants from Haiti and a few Africans from Zaire. All this strongly suggests that an infectious agent is the cause of this disease and that this can be transferred by sexual activity or by the use of blood or blood products.

Cases have been reported in many countries throughout the world, and the mortality rate is very high. To date (August 1984) more than 4,000 patients with the illness have been reported in the USA and 62 in the UK, but it should be stressed that in Britain, AIDS is still a very rare disease and in whatever country of the world it appears, it is most commonly seen in bisexual and homosexual men and intravenous drug abusers. Spread by heterosexual relationships is extremely rare. If a virus is found to be the cause, then blood tests to diagnose the existence of the illness should soon be developed and this could be followed by eventual development of an anti-viral vaccine.

In 1984 doctors in the USA and France isolated a virus from patients with AIDS. This virus is known in France as the 'Lymphadenopathy Associated Virus' (LAV) and in America as 'Human T Cell Leukaemia Virus type 3' (HTLV3). It seems likely that these two viruses will be shown to be identical and to be the cause of AIDS.*

*Details of a British medical study were reported in the medical journal, *The Lancet* on 31 August 1984. Doctors in London and Manchester had studied blood samples from 2,000 people for traces of the virus HTLV3 and had found signs of it in ninety-seven per cent of patients suffering from AIDS. They found signs of this virus not only in AIDS sufferers but in their sexual contacts, homosexuals, haemophiliacs and a small number of people who injected themselves with drugs. The study also gave some assurance as to the low risk at present of acquiring HTLV3 infection or AIDS by blood transfusion in Britain. One of the doctor-authors of the study was reported in the *Daily Telegraph* 1 September 1984 to have said that homosexuals should limit the number of their partners: 'If you sleep around you stand a much higher chance of infection from the virus; it is as simple as that. We are not making any moral judgements, just pointing out medical facts'.

Intense medical research is going on in many countries and reports will undoubtedly appear at frequent intervals.

ORGANISM		DISEASE
Spirochaetes	Treponema pallidum	Syphilis
Bacteria	Neisseria gonorrhoea	Gonorrhoea
	Haemophilus ducreyi	Chancroid
	Donovania	Granuloma inquinale
	Chlamydia trachomatis	(50% of non-gonococcal urethritis) (Lymphogranuloma)
	Gardnerella vaginalis	Gardnerella vaginitis
Viruses	Herpes simplex virus 1 & 2	Herpes
	Pox virus	Molluscum contagiosum
	Papillama virus	Genital warts
	Hepatitis B virus	Hepatitis B
Fungi	Candida albicans	*Moniliasis
	Epidermophyton inguinale	Tinea cruris (ringworm)
Protogoa	Trichomonas vaginalis	Trichomoniasis
Parasites	Sarcoptes scabiei	*Scabies
	Phthirius pubis	Pediculosis pubis
Unknown		about 50% of non-specific urethritis

*Can be transmitted by other than sexual contact

CHAPTER XI

Women's health questions
and WHC answers

The Women's Health Concern mailbag constantly contains letters from women who seem to be unable to ask their own doctors about problems which they cannot understand. They would like to have reliable information on many topics, but often fail, apparently, to elicit clear responses from their doctors.

WHC's medical advisers have devoted a great deal of time to replying to many such women personally in the hope that it will help both them and many others. Some of these questions and replies are quoted in this chapter precisely to provide that kind of guidance to the reader.

Pre- and post-operative worries

I was sterilised three-and-a-half years ago by laparoscopy and in June I became pregnant. An ectopic pregnancy was suspected and both fallopian tubes were removed. The experience was emotionally traumatic and physically extremely painful . . . I explained to the gynaecologist that I had very heavy periods after the sterilisation and was informed that this can be a side-effect . . . I am absolutely horrified that information about the possible effect on menstruation seems not normally to be divulged and that hysterectomy should then be offered as a means of birth control . . . women need to know more facts so that they can make a free choice about whether or not to be sterilised.

THE WHC REPLY WAS:

Failure of a sterilisation operation to prevent pregnancy is bound to be a very upsetting experience for a woman and leave her angry. It is unfortunately a possible outcome, even though a rare one. Heavier periods after tubal ligation for sterilisation is also a recognised possible complication and should be mentioned by the gynaecologist at the time of recommending sterilisation. Hysterectomy, rather than tubal ligation, is a reasonable procedure for the older woman who is certain she does not want to have (or should not have) a further pregnancy and who has had menstrual problems or is known to have uterine disease, such as fibroids; it eliminates the risk of cancer of the uterus (cervix and body) and of menorrhagia before the menopause. It is, of course, more risky than laparoscopic tubal ligation and therefore less easily justified for a woman

127

with an apparently normal uterus. All aspects of contraception should be properly discussed by patients with their doctors before a final choice is made jointly.

Two months ago I went to hospital for the removal of the right-hand Bartholin gland* which was abcessed. I had been seeing my doctor for five months previously for pain in the vaginal area . . . by the time he identified the problems anti-biotics were no help and I was told that surgery was the only answer. At the same time I had a cervical polyp removed and a dilatation and curettage (D & C) and everything was found to be normal . . . but I am still suffering a lot of pain and discomfort.

WHC REPLY:
The successful operation on a Bartholin's abcess, after healing, should leave no pain at all. The persistence of pain on the operated side and the presence of pain on the other side, indicates that all is not well and you should certainly have further gynaecological examination. If you are dissatisfied with what has happened in the hands of the gynaecologist to whom you were referred you are entitled to ask your doctor to refer you to a different gynaecologist, explaining what has already happened and why his/her help is now being sought.

Pending a hysterectomy, I found my doctor unsympathetic and now my husband has hurt me also . . . we are both concerned it might affect our sex lives . . . he is worried that I might suddenly become old, less feminine and have less sex drive . . . all this had not occurred to me before and worries me . . . also will my PMS problems disappear after the operation?

WHC REPLY:
Go and talk to the gynaecologist who will do your operation. Very probably you should have a hysterectomy. Once you are fully recovered, there is no reason why your sex life should not be as good as ever. PMS symptoms do recur after hysterectomy and you should be able to get appropriate treatment for this. Whether you have menopause symptoms and when cannot be predicted. If you get them you should ask for treatment – if you do not get them, you may not need any treatment.

Nine years ago when I had my daughter I had a dermoid ovarian cyst. They said it was not serious but I have a friend who had to have a similar cyst removed. Does this mean I should have mine removed and how will I know if it needs to be removed? Also I have a prolapse of the womb. I have had this for five years with no trouble.

---

*Bartholin's glands: two small glands which secrete mucus on either side at the back of the two outer lips (labia majora) of the vaginal opening. They sometimes become infected and swollen.

WHC REPLY:
Though dermoid cysts are usually not dangerous, it is common practice to remove them to be on the safe side. As you also have a prolapse you should ask your doctor to refer you to a gynaecologist for an opinion on whether either or both of these conditions ought to be treated.

Treatments

My doctor gave me Duphaston and I felt extremely well while taking it but unfortunately I developed a breast lump. It was non-malignant but my doctor now refuses to give me any hormone treatment . . . I feel this is the only answer to my problems.

WHC REPLY:
The finding of a non-malignant lump in the breast is not a reason for discontinuing Duphaston if hitherto it had been helping your premenstrual symptoms. In fact, taking progestogen is more likely to prevent the development of similar lumps. The Oxford study of women using oral contraceptives (which contain progestogens, not unlike Duphaston) has shown that the women have significantly less benign breast disease than non-users.

My doctor asked me if I would be prepared to try 'synflex' tablets which contain naproxen sodium. They are normally used for people with arthritis but my doctor had found them successful for some women who suffer period pains . . . I have taken this drug for two months now and have been relatively free from pain which before was so severe that I had to take time off work . . . can you tell me how and why it works?

WHC REPLY:
Naproxen is a prostaglandin synthetase inhibitor – it reduces the production of prostaglandin which is believed to be responsible for some, but not all, kinds of period pain. It is quite well known that this type of treatment is helpful for period pains.

I suffer badly from PMT and dysmenorrhoea and have seen a gynaecologist who told me my trouble is due to hormones and may be partly psychological but there is no physical abnormality . . . my doctor has tried to help me with various treatments but without much success and he has now suggested a drug called Danazol might help but he explained it would stop my periods for six months . . . I need to know more about Danazol . . . I want more than six months' relief from my suffering . . . I have written to the PMT clinic near here but they have a long waiting list . . . I am 41 and too old to take the pill . . . I can't suffer my problems much longer.

WHC REPLY:
Danazol is a medication which can reduce or stop the production of oestrogen (female hormone secreted in the ovaries). If taken in sufficient amount the periods will cease. But to treat PMS, smaller doses which do not stop the periods altogether, may be sufficient to control the symptoms. A trial of 100 mg daily, only increasing it if it is ineffective at that dose, can usually be made without side-effects and at the low dose this treatment can be continued as long as necessry.

Conditions

Can you give me information on the polycystic ovary syndrome, please?

WHC REPLY:
The polycystic ovary syndrome consists of menstrual disturbance (delayed or absent periods) with enlargement of the ovaries due to the presence of numerous cystic follicles. In some cases there is growth of unwanted hair and in some there is obesity. The cause is not known for certain but is believed to depend upon disturbed hormonal relationships between the ovaries and the pituitary gland with the adjacent part of the brain (hypothalamus) to which it is functionally connected. As a consequence, the ovaries tend to produce more male hormones and less female hormones than they should. Failure of ovulation and hence infertility is usually the case.

Is it true that I cannot become pregnant with a retroversion of the womb?

WHC REPLY:
No, retroversion is not a cause of infertility. Further tests are necessary . . .

I am only sixteen and do not wish to go on the pill yet . . . I have varicose veins and need to know more about them and if they would respond to injections . . . Can you give me any leaflets on the woman's body as all teenagers worry about things and if everything is OK with them inside . . .

WHC REPLY:
Varicose veins are not necessarily a contra-indication to oral contraception. They can be treated by injections but not in all cases. Your doctor can certainly advise whether treatment is needed – it is hardly ever required in 16-year-old girls. The FPA information service can supply free leaflets to you and your friends on birth control and related matters. (Address included at end of this book).

Can you please tell me what placebo tablets are and what they do?

WHC REPLY:
Placebo tablets include inactive substances which pass through the body

with no biological effect and they often provide useful psychological treatment for some of those who fear, without actual cause, they may be suffering from some physical condition. If symptoms are due to actual disease these may persist until an appropriate medicine or procedure is administered. These 'dummy tablets' are also used in double-blind controlled clinical trials for evaluating the effectiveness of medical treatments. The two types of tablets look exactly the same and in many clinical trials the placebo effects are pronounced and interesting. Those who suffer physical symptoms, however, get little or no relief from placebos whereas they get significant effect from *effective* drugs.

Anorexia nervosa and Bulimia

One of the most distressing psychological disturbances with far-reaching physical problems is *anorexia nervosa*. It is suffered mainly by young women and is a form of self-imposed starvation. Seeing a daughter, sister or friend in this situation can be a very worrying experience. The victim is not easy to help as she is usually contradictory, secretive and unwilling to talk honestly about her perverse behaviour with anyone. However, increasing publicity on the subject has brought countless calls to WHC from many people who realise the possible dangers and those who say *they* need to do something about it before it is too late.

Under-eating is only the beginning of the many troubles that can develop sooner or later. For instance, periods disappear if a woman is too under-nourished and eventually it becomes difficult, if not impossible, for her to eat anything at all. In extreme cases fatal diseases can develop.

One attractive young actress said she had gone without food in the first place because she was utterly frustrated by her lack of success in finding the parts she longed to play. Many girls admitted they wanted to stay slim like the models who are photographed wearing revealing bathing suits and fashionable clothes. Many had personal anxieties that had caused them deep depression and they needed urgent psychiatric treatment.

The practice of eating excessively and then vomiting before the food has time to digest to keep weight down is known as *Bulimia* – 'bingeing and puking'. Hundreds of women have asked WHC for advice , such as the following inquiry:

After reading an article on bulimia I am writing to you in the hope that you may be able to help my friend and me . . . we have suffered for two years and have both attended a psychologist which helped to a certain degree . . . but we still need further information and perhaps group therapy. Can you please help?'

WHC REPLY:
Bulimia means an excessive – even voracious – appetite. Rarely it may be caused by an insulin-secreting tumour of the pancreas. Most commonly

there is no evidence of an organic cause and emotional factors are believed to be responsible – the reverse picture to anorexia nervosa.

Many women suffer from the 'Daisy Dustbin Syndrome'. They eat family leftovers or indulge in constant eating because they have stresses or are bored with their lives. It is rather like drinking or smoking too much. They need to establish new eating patterns and a balanced diet to maintain good health.

There is nothing new about 'bingeing and puking'. More than 2,000 years ago the Romans induced vomiting as a social practice after they had indulged in heavy eating. Taking laxatives after heavy eating is also dangerous. Both practices can lead to health hazards.

If you cannot come to terms with this problem for yourself – see your doctor first and be honest when you explain the problem and ask for a referral to a psychotherapist. Group therapy can be useful if you can find the right therapist.

Compulsive eaters are also beset with emotional and physical problems that go far beyond any question of over-weight. These include hypertertension, diabetes, hernia, arthritis and heart disease. WHC always tries to help them, and occasionally our efforts are rewarded by a letter such as this:

About eighteen months ago I spoke to you asking where I could go to help myself with a compulsive eating problem.

You suggested I might see a psychotherapist. I have seen her every week since then and I should like to say what a worthwhile process this has proved to be. She has helped me in coping with depression and all its concomitant symptoms.

Conclusion – Treatment now and in the future

Progress towards better health care involves many factors and it will take considerable time to resolve them to everyone's advantage. A prime requirement is for people to be better educated to help themselves properly and to make effective use of the services available to them.

Drug compliance

Drug compliance means taking the medicines prescribed. Non-compliance has become an expensive and widespread worry, and little has been done to help the public understand its significance. Sometimes ignorance and mistrust of the treatments they are prescribed cause patients not to comply and many expensive drugs are poured down the lavatory. The biggest drawback, however, is that most non-compliers are people who seldom bother to take care of themselves anyway. Unless treatments are taken correctly there can be dire results – for instance, if a woman forgets to take her contraceptive pills or just takes one whenever she feels like it, instead of following the regular pattern of instruction that is shown on every pack, she is very likely to become pregnant. Even if she is taking a morning-after-pill she must do so on time! When their lives depend on taking treatments seriously patients are more likely to follow instructions than in the case of other treatments, like psychotropic prescriptions, which are prescribed for anxiety and family problems.

It is fair to point out, however, that instructions are not always written clearly on pill containers. Simple instructions should always be printed boldly and clearly. Doctors have not only to reaffirm correct drug dosage and then encourage and sustain patients' compliance, but they should also detect failure to comply. Often it is necessary for them to involve a member of the family or a friend (if they exist) in helping to supervise treatment. Some patients are unable to cope with regular pill-taking, especially if this is for lengthy periods of time. Long-acting psychotropic drugs are often given by injection precisely because the dose can be regulated by the doctor or nurse each time it is administered.

The need for better health education

Health education has not yet been taken seriously enough in Britain. We are told that 30 per cent of the population is unable to understand even the simplest and most clearly written pamphlets. Many schools apparently choose not to find time for existing programmes that would involve only one twenty-minute session a week throughout school life. We are also given to understand that existing educational pamphlets rarely reach children in social groups four and five who are the ones who need them the most. Things cannot improve, therefore, until health educators are trained to communicate simple, correct information to all fit children from the age of five. It is no good using teachers who know their other subjects well but may not have trained in health care and are unable to put facts over in a way that is attractive and meaningful to young audiences. Surely it should be national policy to improve the extent and the standard of the nation's health education at all levels? Many people still fail to understand what their doctors are saying to them when they use quite ordinary words, such as acute, abdomen, nutrients, swab or constipation.

Existing differences in the quality of general practice

There seems to be a stark contrast, at present, between the services that are provided by doctors in well organised and well run group practices – and the way in which some other practices seem to cause patients much distress. The art of general practice requires the identification of those who are unequivocally ill. Doctors often say that these patients are usually the least demanding while others try to obtain more and more attention. They say that they spend more time on matters which are not, strictly speaking, medical at all and that a great deal of money is wasted giving people what they demand rather than what is appropriate for them.

Doctors and patients are affected by a range of different attitudes on medical aims and on how the National Health Service should be functioning. More and more the kind of treatment you receive from your General Practitioner seems to depend not only on your ability to explain your symptoms properly but also your knowledge of common health problems. People who are inarticulate and ill-informed are more likely to be troubled by what they see as 'God-like' attitudes in their doctors' authority and complain that they are unable to discuss anything with the doctor. Some complain of brusque dismissal by doctors who seem to ignore the very existence of the problems from which they are suffering. They also say that they are not told anything about the treatment prescribed or the operations considered to be necessary. They themselves usually fail to ask the doctors the questions they wish to have answered and many end up receiving no treatment at all or the wrong treatment. Most people learn to cope with everyday stresses and strains but when physical illness also occurs they need reliable help from facilities that should be available to them from their family doctors or from specialised clinics. 'Holistic medicine' describes what good doctors have always been doing and all others should have been doing: looking at the health of the *whole* person and not just at the illness itself when a patient presents himself or herself for assessment and medical advice. The problem is that good doctors and facilities are not equally available for everyone who needs them.

A revolutionary policy

The Royal College of General Practitioners (RCGP) is evolving a new policy which, they hope, will improve the services provided by General Practitioners in NHS practices. They have established a Patients' Liaison Group which will enable patients' representatives to discuss problems in GP services so that going 'straight to the horse's mouth' might start to effect the changes that are needed.

The RCGP is well aware of the difficulties that arise for many people who receive inadequate attention when they visit their doctors and the unacceptable differences in quality of general practice that persist. Poor care is often the result of a General Practitioner's apparent incompetence or unwillingness to provide a good basic health service. Dr Donald Irvine, Chairman of the Council, commented at length on outstanding problems and the quality of care in general practice in the RCGP Journal.*

> As a College we are required to address the problem of quality with a new sense of urgency, determination and purpose . . . Our foremost challenge is to provide primary and continuing medical care of a standard which will be regarded as not merely acceptable but highly desirable by the community at large . . . If we fail to tackle the quality issue thoroughly and decisively now, forces outside and around general practice could move quite quickly, singly or in concert to undermine our foundations even if we can demonstrate large pockets of success through examples of good practice . . .

Dr Irvine outlined a scenario of alternative options to be taken very seriously by all doctors and added:

> In our pursuit of quality we can expect help from an increasingly articulate and discerning public which is encouraged to question the quality of our service by special interest groups and the media. Such questioning should be welcomed for it provides a much needed customer stimulus even though it may expose weaknesses with a degree of precision and frankness to which we are not accustomed.

He concluded:

> We should now adopt a policy that can turn hopes into reality in the

*August 1983; Volume 33, no 253.

next five years within the College and in ten years within general practice as a whole.

Services in NHS General Practices

Dr William Styles, Honorary Secretary of the RCGP, is involved in initiatives designed to improve the primary care services in Britain. He and his colleagues are encouraging doctors to be more receptive to the problems that are brought to them and to discuss treatments and suggested arrangements properly with their patients. He says that, nowadays, doctors' training includes all the know-how that is necessary for them to treat the many problems they are asked to deal with in their surgeries or to refer them to good specialists. There are postgraduate training schemes for doctors to keep them up-to-date with new developments, techniques and treatments, and emphasis is being placed on 'how to talk and listen to your patients'. Patient participation is also recommended in certain practice activities.

A number of good NHS practices already exist which are efficient and effective. Many of them provide well-women clinic services and all GP surgeries should be augmented to do the same. A typical practice team might include doctors, health visitors, district nurses, a midwife, receptionists and secretaries. In many surgeries, women who prefer to see a woman doctor can do so.

Health visitors help mothers with young children as well as people of all ages to cope with their problems. District nurses provide daily treatments at the practices and visit those who are ill in their homes. The community midwife sees mothers in their homes before and after their babies are born and organises ante-natal relaxation classes. Communication between doctors and patients is considered of vital importance. Patients cooperate with doctors in helping to teach recently qualified doctors, medical students, health visitors, nurses and receptionists about all aspects of the work that they do.

Some doctors have prepared information leaflets about their practices which describe the services provided and explain fully how to arrange surgery consultations, house calls and out-of-hours services. There is also a list of services available to those who are well and wish to maintain their good health. This includes weekly clinics for well babies, immunisations for young children, diabetic patients, health checks for the elderly, an ante-natal clinic for pregnant mothers, immunisation against Rubella (German measles) for ten-year-old-girls on request, immunity checks for this disease for women who want to become pregnant and may need vaccination, cervical smears for women of all ages, and blood pressure checks during surgery sessions, also on request. Family planning and contraceptive advice is also given by many doctors. It is always, in fact, worthwhile for patients to find out beforehand what services are offered by NHS general practices, in advance of registering with them.

The National Health Service

If everyone had access to good doctors and was able to visit them with confidence and without fear the overall scene could be greatly improved. But it is not just a question of developing good relations between doctors and those who need them. The better educated are usually able to take care of themselves and use whatever is best in the services provided while the ill-educated, weak or elderly often remain unable to take sensible advantage of the facilities available. This situation could exist forever unless it is taken more seriously by society itself and, in particular, by all those who are involved in the health care delivery services. A widespread and genuine effort would have to be made to co-ordinate their policies and work – from the government departments responsible for health and social services, the environment, water and sewerage, housing and education, employment and industry, to the countless committees and groups in local government and elsewhere which try to deal with health and community affairs.

The amount of national expenditure that could be set aside to provide health and social care for the entire population is limited only by the amount the nation is prepared to pay. The cost of the services, technology, equipment and treatment seems continually to forge ahead of the money that is allotted for the treatment of the sick and the provision of better services – including health education and public knowledge of available preventive measures – to the public at large. Much good work has been done over the years which must not be overlooked, but there is and always will be criticism of the way in which funds are distributed.

In 1983 the government allocated to the NHS £15½ billion which was derived mostly from taxes, national insurance stamps and prescription charges. Manpower costs accounted for three-quarters of the money spent in running the hospital service. The cost of cleaning, laundry and catering was £900 million. The NHS employed 820,000 people and was the biggest employer in western Europe. This included 105,000 administrators and 170,000 ancillary staff. Those who wanted the government to find more money for the Service argued that other countries were spending much more for similar purposes. Government spokesmen replied that the Health Service must always be looking at how it uses the money that the taxpayer gives to it in order to see if it can give better value and services – above all to the patient.

It is generally believed that too much NHS money has been spent on administrative costs and the wasteful use of certain drugs. Many doctors and nurses have opted out of working in the NHS because they claim that the bureaucratic structures surrounding it, and the petty and damaging behaviour of some of the health workers who were constantly being motivated to strike, prevented them from doing a good job in the front line.

If adequate health care for the nation is to be covered by an efficient national health service it should be obvious that the quality of much of the primary care services must be improved; that good dental services must continue to be available; that hospitals and clinics must be properly equipped and maintained and that there should be enough doctors and nurses and other trained staff to enable them to carry out their work and apply proper treatments and care; that the work of the community health services must be carried out by sufficient numbers of trained nurses and others to help the people in their homes who cannot look after themselves.

Caring for the elderly and the disadvantaged

In 1983 there were 3¼ million people in Britain over the age of seventy-five – it is expected in 1993 that there will be nearly four million in that age group. An increasing number of elderly people – particularly women – are faced with loneliness and suffering in their last years because of inadequate care and home help and the acute shortage of properly set-up homes for them. A comparative few have managed to find enough money, usually from £65 to £300 each week to live in privately-run homes. If they are unable to afford the fees and have less than £3,000 left in their savings some of them have managed to get subsidies from social security benefits that have sometimes brought poor or doubtful surroundings for them. Old people in some countries have done better than this – for instance, in Denmark and Finland. Surely *all* old people are worthy of good health care in any caring society?

There should also be more professional help for handicapped people and for children who are sick or unwanted and for those who are mentally ill. Many of the long-suffering carers of relatives and friends – usually women in their own homes – have suffered physical, mental and emotional strains themselves that have stretched their patience and sympathy to the limit.

Some of the voluntary organisations and charities that have proved their worth in the national scene and have often provided answers that have led to national reform should also be given more financial support. Most of them still have to 'beg' for money. Government money should also be allocated more freely to fund medical research. It is little known outside medical circles how most research workers in hospitals and those who are doing post-graduate studies are deprived of proper funding. They have to depend on all kinds of hand-outs from fund-granting agencies including pharmaceutical companies, and there is very considerable competition for these limited funds. Not enough attention has been focused on the fact that their research work is responsible for getting to the roots of the causes of serious diseases and possible treatments for them, as well as conditions which are not likely to be fatal but nevertheless cause widespread suffering and public inconvenience. And this particularly includes the illnesses that affect women.

The NHS has achieved enormous success since its inception in 1948 as compared with the conditions that existed for many people in Britain before its time. Its progress must not be jeopardised by lack of funds or defective management. It is generally believed that a publicly financed health service still offers the best means of achieving an even distribution of available resources to all sections of the community and especially to the under-privileged.

Providing more of us take the trouble to care properly for ourselves, the NHS will survive and its services will be improved out of recognition for all of us who need them.

Appendixes

1. USEFUL ADDRESSES

a) United Kingdom
b) International
c) Establishments where treatment is available for menopause problems in United Kingdom, Eire, Australia and New Zealand.

2. AUTHORS OF WHC BOOKLETS

3. INDEX

Useful Addresses

a) United Kingdom

In Britain, information about local facilities can be obtained from three main sources:

Department of Health and Social Security (see telephone directories for office addresses) will provide details of NHS services, a variety of leaflets and details of Family Practitioner Committees;

Local Health Authorities can supply lists of General Practitioners, health visitors, dentists, opticians, chiropodists and other health practitioners; and addresses of cytology and family planning clinics, details of hospitals and other recognised health centres;

Public Libraries also have information about hospital and clinic facilities; doctors' lists; social services; community health schemes and legal aid; local MPs; women's organisations and groups; further education courses and colleges; and sport and leisure activities.

In the list which follows every effort has been made to ensure accuracy in the names and addresses up to the time of going to press; but the reader will appreciate that changes inevitably occur.

ACCEPT (The *A*lcoholism *C*ommunity for *E*ducation *P*revention and *T*reatment)
Western Hospital
Seagrave Road, London SW6
01-381 3155

ACTION ON ALCOHOL ABUSE
see under Royal College of Physicians

ACUPUNCTURE ASSOCIATION
34 Alderney Street
London SW1 4EU
01-834 3353 and 01-834 1012

AGE CONCERN, England
Bernard Sunley House
60 Pitcairn Road
Mitcham, Surrey. CR4 3LL
01-640 5341

AGE CONCERN, Scotland
33 Castle Street
Edinburgh, EH2 3DN
031-225 5000/1

ALCOHOLICS ANONYMOUS
PO Box 514
11 Redcliffe Gardens
London SW10 9BQ
01-352 9779

ALEXANDER TECHNIQUE
Society of Teachers
38 Albert Court
Prince Consort Road
London SW7
01-589 3834

ANGLO-EUROPEAN COLLEGE OF
CHIROPRACTIC
13 Parkwood Road
Bournemouth
0202-431021

ARTHRITIS AND RHEUMATISM
COUNCIL FOR RESEARCH (ARC)
8–10 Charing Cross Road
London WC2
01-240 0871

ASH (*Action on Smoking and Health*)
5–11 Mortimer Street
London W1
01-637 9843

BIRTH CONTROL CAMPAIGN
27–35 Mortimer Street
London W1A 4QW
01-580 9360

BRITISH DIABETIC ASSOCIATION
10 Queen Anne Street
London W1M 0BD
01-323 1531

BRITISH EPILEPSY ASSOCIATION
New Wokingham Road
Wokingham, Berks RG11 3AY
03446-3122

BRITISH HEART FOUNDATION
57 Gloucester Place
London W1H 4DH
01-935 0185

BRITISH HOMOEOPATHIC
ASSOCIATION
27A Devonshire Street
London W1N 1RJ
01-935 2163

BRITISH MEDICAL ASSOCIATION
(BMA)
Tavistock Square
London WC1
01-387 4499

BRITISH PREGNANCY ADVISORY
SERVICE (BPAS)
Head Office:
Austry Manor
Wootton Wawen
Solihul
West Midlands B95 6DA
056-42 3225

London Office:
58 Petty France
London SW1
01-222 0985

BRITISH SCHOOL OF
OSTEOPATHY
16 Buckingham Gate
London SW1
01-828 9478/9

BROOK ADVISORY CENTRES
(BAC)
233 Tottenham Court Road
London W1P 9AE
01-580 2911 and 01-323 1522
(Contraception, pregnancy, psycho-
sexual problems)

BUPA (The *British United Provident
Association*)
Battle Bridge House
300 Gray's Inn Road
London WC1X 8DU
01-837 6484

CAPITAL RADIO Help Line
01-388 7575

CITIZEN'S ADVICE BUREAUX,
National Association of
110 Drury Lane
London WC28 5SW
01-836 9231
(825 Citizen's Advice Bureaux in
Britain)

CITIZEN'S RIGHTS OFFICE
1 Macklin Street
Drury Lane
London WC28 5NH
01-405 5942/4517

CONSUMER'S ASSOCIATION (CA)
14 Buckingham Street
London WC2N 6DS
01-839 1222
(*Publishers of WHICH magazine*)

COUNCIL AND CARE FOR THE
ELDERLY
131 Middlesex Street
London E1 7JF
01-621 1624

DEPARTMENT OF HEALTH AND
SOCIAL SECURITY (DHSS)
Alexander Fleming House
Elephant and Castle
London SE1 6BY
01-407 5522
(Government department for central
planning of the NHS)

ELIZABETH GARRETT ANDERSON
HOSPITAL (EGA), The
144 Euston Road
London NW1
01-387 2501

ENDOMETRIOSIS SOCIETY, The
65 Holmdene Avenue
London SE14 9LD
01-737 4764

FAMILY PLANNING
ASSOCIATION, (FPA) The
27–35 Mortimer Street
London W1N 7RJ
01-636 7866

(FAMILY PLANNING
INFORMATION SERVICE at same
address – free publications list)

FAWCETT SOCIETY
46 Harleyford Road
London SE11 5AY
01-587 1287
(Long established society for equal
rights movement. Contact: Women's
Health Committee)

GINGERBREAD
Minerva Chambers
35 Wellington Street
London WC2E 7BN
01-240 0953
(one-parent families)

HEALTH EDUCATION COUNCIL
78 New Oxford Street
London WC1A 1AH
01-637 1881

HELP THE AGED
32 Dover Street
London W1A 2AP
01-499 0972

HERPES ASSOCIATION
c/o Spare Rib
27 Clerkenwell Close
London EC1 DAT

INSTITUTE FOR
COMPLEMENTARY MEDICINE
21 Portland Place
London W1N 3AF
01-636 9543

INSTITUTE OF PSYCHO-SEXUAL
MEDICINE, The
11 Chandos Street
London W1
01-580 1043

JOHN GROOMS ASSOCIATION
FOR THE DISABLED
10 Gloucester Drive
Finsbury Park
London N4 2LP
01-802 7272

MARIE STOPES CLINIC
Well Woman Centre
108 Whitfield Street
London WC1P 6BE
01-388 0662 *and* 01-388 2585

MARRIAGE GUIDANCE COUNCIL
76A New Cavendish Street
London W1
01-580 1087

MEDICAL COUNCIL ON
ALCOHOLISM LIMITED
3 Grosvenor Crescent
London SQ1X 7EE
01-235 4182

MENCAP (Mentally *H*andicapped
Children)
123 Golden Lane
London EC1Y 0RT
01-253 9433

MIGRAINE TRUST
45 Great Ormonde Street
London WC1N 3HD
01-278 2676
Note: The NHS provides facilities in
The Princess Margaret Migraine
Clinic, Charing Cross Hospital,
Fulham Palace Road, London W6)

MIND
22 Harley Street
London W1
01-637 0741)
(National Association for mental
health)

MULTI ETHNIC WOMENS HEALTH
PROJECT
C/o City & Hackney CHC
210 Kingsland Road
London E2 8EB
(non-English speaking women)

NATIONAL CHILDBIRTH TRUST
9 Queensborough Terrace
London W2 3TB
01-221 3833

NATIONAL COUNCIL OF SOCIAL
SERVICES
26 Bedford Square
London WC1B 3HU
01-636 4066

NATIONAL FEDERATION OF
WOMENS INSTITUTES (NFWI)
39 Eccleston Street
London SW1W 9NT
01-730 7212
(9,184 WI's in England and Wales)

NATIONAL WOMEN'S AID
FEDERATION
374 Grays Inn Road
London WC1
01-837 9316
(helps battered women and children)

OPEN LINE TO HELP
St Martin-in-the-Fields
Trafalgar Square
London WC2
01-930 1732

PARKINSON'S DISEASE SOCIETY
36 Portland Place
London W1N 3DG
01-323 1174

PATIENTS' ASSOCIATION
11 Dartmouth Street
London SW1H 9BN
01-222 4992

POST NATAL ILLNESS The
Association for,
7 Gowan Avenue
London SW6

PREGNANCY ADVISORY SERVICE
40 Margaret Street
London W1N 7FB
01-409 0281

PPP MEDICAL CENTRE
(*Private Patients' Plan*)
Tavistock Square, London WC1
01-388 2468

PSYCHOTHERAPY CENTRE
67 Upper Berkeley Street
London W1
01-262 8852

RAPE CRISIS
PO Box 42
London N6 5BU
01-340 6913

RELAXATION FOR LIVING
29 Burwood Park Road
Walton-on-Thames
Surrey
98-27861

RELEASE
1 Elgin Avenue
London W9
01-289 1123
(drug addiction, abortion, housing and
immigration problems)

ROYAL COLLEGE OF GENERAL
PRACTITIONERS (RCGP), The
14 Princes Gate
London SW7
01-581 3232

ROYAL COLLEGE OF
OBSTETRICIANS AND
GYNAECOLOGISTS, The
27 Sussex Place
London NW1
01-262 5425

ROYAL COLLEGE OF PHYSICIANS,
The
11 St Andrews Place
London NW1
01-935 1174

ACTION ON ALCOHOL ABUSE
(AAA)
Usher Institute
Warrender Park Road
Edinburgh EH9
(Started in 1983, supported by The
Royal College of Physicians.)

ROYAL COLLEGE OF SURGEONS,
THE
Lincoln's Inn Fields
London WC2A 3PN
01-405 6507

ROYAL LONDON
HOMOEOPATHIC HOSPITAL, The
Great Ormonde Street
London W1
01-837 3091
(centre for alternative medicine)

SAMARITANS, The
17 Uxbridge Road
Slough SL1 1SN
0753-32713

SPASTICS SOCIETY
12 Park Crescent
London W1N 4EQ
01-636 5020

STRESS SYNDROME
FOUNDATION, The
Cedar House
Yalding, Kent
ME18 6JD
0622-814431

TERRENCE HIGGINS TRUST
Limited, The
BM AIDS,
London WC1N 3XX
01-278 8745
(A registered charity to inform, advise
and help on AIDS)

WESTMINSTER HOSPITAL
Genito-Urinary Medicine
(special clinic)
Department OP6
Dean Ryle Street
Horseferry Road, London SW1
01-630 5266
(sex problems and infections)

147

WOMEN'S NATIONAL CANCER
CONTROL CAMPAIGN (WNCCC)
1 South Audley Street
London W1Y 5DG
01-499 7532/4

YOUNG PEOPLE'S COUNSELLING
SERVICE
Tavistock Clinic
Tavistock Centre
120 Belsize Lane
London NW3 5BA
01-435 7111 Ext. 327
(age 16 upwards)

International addresses

International Planned Parenthood
Federation
18–20 Lower Regent Street
London SW1Y 4PW
01-839 2911

The World Health Organisation
(WHO)
1211 Geneva 27
Switzerland

United States of America

*Sources of help and information for
women*

Planned Parenthood Federation of
America Inc.
810 7th Avenue
New York, NY 10019

US National Women's Health
Network
224 7th Street SE
Washington DC 2000-3
(202) 543 9222
(Five State Groups)

Women's Health Research Institute
8 Hull Street
Boston, MA 02113
(617) 523 2668

Australia

The Australian Federation of Family
Planning Associations
Suite 603, 6th Floor
Roden Cutler House
24 Campbell Street
Sydney, NSW 2000

New Zealand

The New Zealand Family Planning
Association
PO Box 68-200
214 Karangahape Road
Newton
Auckland 1

Canada

Planned Parenthood
71 Bank Street
Suite 502
Ottawa Ont. K1 PS NS

Belgium

International Health Foundation (IHF)
Naames Straat
43 Rue de Namur
Brussels 1000
02/512 4017

Italy

Isis Italy
Via S. Maria dell'Anima 30
00186 Roma
06/65 65 842

Switzerland

Isis Switzerland
Case Postale 50
CH-1211 Geneva 2
022/33 67 46

(Women's *I*nternational *I*nformation
and Communication *S*ervice)

Medical establishments where treatment is available for menopause problems

Britain

Please note that these lists are intended to help women and doctors to seek the whereabouts of specialist medical facilities. Some menopause clinics or gynaecological advice is available in The Departments of Obstetrics and Gynaecology at the following hospitals. Women who attend them need referral notes from their doctors so that appointments can be made.

London – NHS

Chelsea Hospital for Women
Dovehouse Street
London SW3 6LT
01-352 6446

King's College Hospital
Denmark Hill
London SE5 9RS
01-274 6222

Hospital for Women
(Soho Hospital – part of Middlesex
Hospital Group)
Soho Square
London W1V 6JB
01-580 7928

St Thomas' Hospital
London SE1 7EH
01-928 9292

Royal Free Hospital
Pond Street
London NW3 2Q9
01-794 0500

Samaritan Hospital for Women
Marylebone Road
London NW1 5YE
01-402 4211

St George's Hospital
Blackshaw Road
Tooting
London SW17
01-672 1255

Dulwich Hospital
East Dulwich Grove
London SE21 3PT
01-693 3377

England – NHS

Women's Hospital
Professional Unit
Queen Elizabeth Medical Centre
Edgbaston, Birmingham B15 2TG
021 472 1377

Birmingham & Midland Hospital
  for Women
Showall Green Lane
Birmingham 11
021 772 1101

Royal Sussex Hospital
Brighton, Sussex
0273 66611

Dryburn Hospital
Durham
0385 64911

The Lady Chichester Hospital
New Church Street
Hove, Sussex
0273 778383

Beckenham Hospital
379 Croydon Road
Beckenham
Kent
01-650 0125

Women's Hospital
Leeds
0532 453905

The General Infirmary
MRC Mineral Metabolism Unit
Leeds
0532 32799

Women's Hospital
Gynaecological Clinic
Catherine Street
Liverpool
051 709 5461

Wythenshawe Hospital
Southmoor Road
Manchester 22
061 998 7070

Manchester General Hospital
Crumpsall
Manchester M8 6RB
061 740 1444

Mexborough Montagu Hospital
Adwick Road
Mexborough
South Yorkshire
070 988 5171

Newcastle General Hospital
Westgate Road
Newcastle upon Tyne NE4 6BE
0632 38811

City Hospital
Hucknall Road
Nottingham
0602 608111

George Eliot Hospital
College Street
Nuneaton
Warwickshire
0682 384201

The John Radcliffe Hospital
Oxford
0865 64711

Peterborough & District Hospital
Thorpe Road
Peterborough
0733 67451

Jessop Hospital
University Department
Sheffield
0742 25291

Royal Hallamshire Hospital
Glossop Road
Sheffield S10 2JF
0742 26484

Stafford General Infirmary
Stafford
0735 58251

Ashford Hospital
Staines
Middlesex
07842 51188

Stepping Hill Hospital
Stockport
Cheshire
061 483 1010

Scotland – NHS

Aberdeen University
Foresthill
Aberdeen
0244 23423

Royal Infirmary
39 Chalmers Street
Edinburgh EH3 9ER
(Newington) 061 667 1011

Glasgow Royal Infirmary
Castle Street
Glasgow G4 0SF
041 552 3535

Glasgow Western Infirmary
Dunbarton Road
Glasgow G11
041 339 8822

Stobhill Hospital
Balornock Road
Glasgow G21
041 558 0111

Wales – this clinic is not NHS but is free to patients

Simbec Research Centre
Merthyr Tydfil
0685 2324/2533

Northern Ireland – NHS

Samaritan Hospital
Lisburn Road
Belfast
0232 41316

Eire – NHS

Coombe Hospital
Dublin 8
0001 757561

England – Private

London

2 Prince Arthur Road
Hampstead
London NW3 6AU
01-435 4723 (WHC Chairman)

9A Wilbraham Place
Sloane Street
London SW1X 9AL
01-730 7928

56 Harley Street
London W1N 1AE
01-580 6332

BUPA Medical Centre
Battle Bridge House
300 Gray's Inn Road
London WC1X 8DU
01-837 6484

12 Thurloe Street
London SW7
01-584 6204

A gynaecological team at King's
College Hospital provides private
treatment and fees are donated to a
medical research fund
King's College Hospital
Denmark Hill
London SE5 9RS
274 7711 Extn: 2710

20 Church Road
Edgbaston
Birmingham
021 454 2345

The Richmond Hill Clinic
21 Richmond Hill
Clifton
Bristol BS8 18A
0272 736084

32 Westbourne Villas
Hove
Sussex
0273 720217

31 Rodney Street
Liverpool L1 9EH
051 709 8522

Haslemere House
68 Haslemere Avenue
Mitcham
Surrey
01-648 3234

The Nuffield Hospital
Uxborne Avenue
Jesmond
Newcastle upon Tyne
0632 815938

Wavertree Clinic
6 Bradwell Lane
Newcastle
Staffordshire
0782 635218

11 Winmarleigh Street
Warrington WA1 1NB
Lancashire
0925 50705

Women's Private Health Care
Nuffield Nursing Home
Tattenhall
Wolverhampton
Staffordshire
0902 753051

Scotland – Private

Royal Scottish Nursing Home
19 Drumsbaugh Gardens
Edinburgh 3
031 225 3881

The Bellgrove Clinic
556 Gallowgate
Glasgow, G40 2PA
041 554 7157

Eire – Private

15 Mountjoy Square
Dublin 1
0001 744133

42 Butterfield Avenue
Temple
Dublin
0001 900976

Portland House
Greystones
County Wicklow
01-874 308

*FPA clinics providing fee-paying
menopause advice and treatment*

West Midlands FPA Clinic
7 York Road
Birmingham B16 9HX
021 454 0236

Sheffield FPA Clinic
17 North Church Street
Sheffield
0742 21191

Australia

Royal Hospital for Women
188 Oxford Street
Paddington, N.S.W. 2021

King George V Hospital
Missenden Road
Camperdown, N.S.W. 2050

Women's Medical Centre
Suite 80, Challis House
10 Martin Place
Sydney, N.S.W. 2000

Prince Henry's Hospital
St Kilda Road
Melbourne, Vic. 3000

Menstrual-Menopause Clinic
Queen Victoria Medical Centre
Lonsdale Street
Melbourne, Vic. 3000

Psychosomatic Gynaecology Clinic
Royal Melbourne Hospital
Parkville, Vic.

Royal Women's Hospital
Gratten Street
Carlton, Vic. 3053

Flinders Medical Centre
Bedford Park
South Australia 5042

King Edward Memorial Hospital
Bagot Road
Subiaco
Western Australia 6008

The Endocrine Unit
Royal Adelaide Hospital
North Terrace
Adelaide
South Australia 5000

New Zealand

National Women's Hospital
Auckland

Queen Mary Hospital
Dunedin

Family Planning Clinics
in Auckland, Wellington and
Christchurch

Note for 'women at work'
Many of the doctors and occupational
health nurses who work in surgeries in
industrial companies and other
organisations are trained to talk to
women about their menopause and
other cyclic problems.

AUTHORS OF WHC BOOKLETS

Women's Health Concern, as stated in the Author's Preface, publishes a series of booklets on women's health problems. The medical and scientific texts of five of these are included in Chapters VI, VII, VIII, IX and X and the author of each is as follows:

FEMININE HYGIENE by Gerald Swyer MA, DM, MD, DPhil, FRCP, FRCOG
Dr Gerald Swyer is Chairman of Women's Health Concern. He was Director of the Fertility Clinic and Consultant Endocrinologist in the Department of Obstetrics and Gynaecology at University College Hospital in London for thirty-one years, until his retirement from that post in 1978. He remains actively concerned in treating all aspects of women's health problems.

PREMENSTRUAL SYNDROME & PERIOD PAINS by Michael Brush, PhD
Dr Michael Brush is Senior Lecturer in biochemistry in the Department of Obstetrics and Gynaecology at St Thomas' Hospital in London. He has done extensive research work on the use of synthetic hormones, vitamins and dietary supplements for PMS sufferers since 1975.

THE MENOPAUSE by John McQueen, FRCS MRCOG, DCH
Mr John McQueen was a member of the team of gynaecologists at the menopause clinic in the Department of Obstetrics and Gynaecology at the Chelsea Hospital for Women and Queen Charlotte's Maternity Hospital in London for seven years until 1980, when he became a consultant gynaecologist at the Beckenham Hospital in Kent.

POST-NATAL DEPRESSION by Irene Swyer, psychotherapist
Irene Swyer, having trained at the Middlesex Hospital as a radiographer, fulfilled a lifelong interest by training as a psychotherapist only later in life and has since practised privately, mainly in the fields of anxiety and depression. She has a wide experience of the emotional problems associated with interpersonal relationships, inside and outside marriage.

SEXUALLY TRANSMITTED DISEASES by John Kenyon Oates, FRCP (E)
Dr John Kenyon Oates is consultant in genito-urinary medicine at Westminster Hospital in London where he runs Department OP6 which deals with sex problems and diseases. Dr Oates is also consultant in charge of the Department of Genito-Urinary Medicine at Addenbrooke's Hospital in Cambridge.

Index